Managing Moods Workbook for Teens

A TOOLBOX of REPRODUCIBLE ASSESSMENTS and ACTIVITIES for FACILITATORS

Ester R. A. Leutenberg
and John J. Liptak, EdD

Duluth, Minnesota

101 W. 2nd St., Suite 203
Duluth, MN 55802-1908

800-247-6789

books@wholeperson.com
www.wholeperson.com

Managing Moods Workbook for Teens
A Toolbox of Reproducible Assessments and Activities

Copyright ©2014 by Ester R.A. Leutenberg and John J. Liptak. All rights reserved. Except for short excerpts for review purposes and materials in the assessment, journaling activities, and educational handouts sections, no part of this book may be reproduced or transmitted in any form by any means, electronic or mechanical without permission in writing from the publisher. Self-assessments, exercises, and educational handouts are meant to be photocopied.

All efforts have been made to ensure accuracy of the information contained in this book as of the date published. The author(s) and the publisher expressly disclaim responsibility for any adverse effects arising from the use or application of the information contained herein.-

Printed in the United States of America

10 9 8 7 6 5 4 3 2 1

Editorial Director: Carlene Sippola
Art Director: Joy Morgan Dey

Library of Congress Control Number: 2014909596
ISBN: 978-1-57025-320-1

Introduction

Using the *Managing Moods Workbook for Teens*

Teen years can be extremely difficult, even in the best of circumstances. During these years emotions can be intense, and changes in mood occur very rapidly. Adolescence is a time of not only great emotional turmoil, but also sudden mood swings and increasing rebelliousness. It is important for teens to be aware of when they are responding typically to stressful life circumstances or when they are experiencing excessive moodiness that seems to be taking over their lives.

Teens tend to be very emotional. Some of these feelings will be positive. On the other hand, some may also be negative and bring forth feelings of sadness, restlessness and irritability. It is usual to feel these types of negative feelings every now and then, but when these moody feelings last for weeks, months, or even years, it is a sign of a more serious mood issue. When teens find themselves taking little joy in activities they have previously enjoyed, appearing increasingly more irritable, and feeling fatigue and a general loss of energy, they may be experiencing symptoms of more serious problems that require assessment and treatment by a medical professional.

Serious mental health issues can stretch far beyond the usual limits of disappointment, loss, frustration, and joylessness. Mood problems can be accompanied by an inability to cope with everyday life issues and stressors. Rather than temporary feelings of *down in the dumps*, these extreme feelings tend to last for more than a few hours or days and tend to affect all aspects of a teen's life, leaving the teen feeling empty, unable to function as usual, and possibly hopeless for weeks, months, and years.

Teens who experience problems in maintaining a balanced and healthy overall mood are often incapable of functioning well in daily life. They frequently experience extreme emotional states, negative feelings, and self-defeating moods inconsistent with what is happening in their environment. Teens struggling with this mental condition find that they are unable to conquer their moodiness with family members, with family and friends, at school and in their community. Teens experiencing moodiness have problems in interpersonal relationships, ability to study and concentrate, and in the ways they eat, sleep, relax, and live their daily lives. Their real potential is greatly inhibited.

What Other Ways Does a Mood Management Issue Manifest Itself?

For teens, moodiness manifests itself in a wide variety of ways. It is critical to be aware of, understand, and be cognizant of how these symptoms are commonly seen in teens. Although all symptoms to do not have to be present, those that are will typically cause significant distress and/or impairment in daily functioning:

- Restlessness
- Poor school performance
- Irritability
- Argumentative/angry outbursts at home and in the community
- Antisocial behavior
- Running away from home
- Theft and vandalism
- Unsafe sexual behavior
- Secretiveness

- Alcohol/illegal drug use
- Withdrawal
- Bullying
- Picking fights
- Weight gain/weight loss
- Feelings of worthlessness
- Loss of appetite
- Pronounced fears and phobias
- Family Upheaval
- Fatigue

- Inability to think, focus, or make decisions
- Loss of interest in activities and/or people
- Problems exaggerated or imaginary
- Self-mutilation
- Preoccupation with death and/or suicide
- Physical complaints – excessive/exaggerated

**Our goal for this workbook is NOT to diagnose a mental illness,
or even for the facilitator to make that diagnosis from this book's content.**
Please see page x for further explanation.

Types of Serious Mood Inconsistencies

Different types of mood disturbances are conveyed and expressed in different forms and include:

MAJOR DEPRESSION (often referred to as unipolar depression) involves a profoundly sad mood and a high probability of distorted depressive thinking that occur over time.
Some of the additional symptoms:
- A persistent, sad mood most of the day accompanied by feeling empty
- Experiencing a significant reduction in appetite and weight loss when not dieting, or increased appetite and weight gain
- Hypersomnia (sleeping too much) or insomnia (an inability to sleep)
- Feelings of inadequacy
- Racing thoughts and impulsive behaviors
- Hostility or aggression
- Feelings of agitation or feelings of restlessness
- Fatigue, loss of energy or feelings of being slowed down
- Feelings of worthlessness and hopelessness or excessive or inappropriate guilt
- Diminished ability to think or concentrate, remember things or be decisive
- Constant feelings of anxiety or feelings of irritability
- Loss of interest in activities, or a decrease in pleasure in activities once enjoyed
- Physical symptoms such as headaches, pain, digestive problems
- Thoughts of suicide and/or causing danger to others

BIPOLAR DEPRESSION involves an alteration (like a roller-coaster ride) of down feelings (depression) and up feelings (excessive and often inappropriate euphoric), rapid speech and hyperactivity.
Some additional symptoms:
- Cycles of elation and depression
- Distinct periods of abnormally and persistently elevated and euphoric mood
- Inflated self-esteem or grandiosity
- Decrease in the need for sleep
- Flight of ideas
- Distractibility
- Increased engagement in risky behavior

MILDER FORMS OF DEPRESSION carry detectable symptoms and impact daily activities in ways that demonstrate a diminished interest in things people usually find interesting or enjoyable.
Some of these types of mood disturbances:
- Dysthymia – Person has a mild depression that lingers for more than two years. For people with dysthymia, life has little pleasure. They tend to be cranky, irritable, and testy.
- Postpartum Depression – Person experiences depression after childbirth. Sometimes called *baby blues*, this type of depression may be associated with psychological and physical factors.
- Seasonal Affective Disorder – Person experiences depression with seasonal changes in climate and light.

DEPRESSION FROM UNKNOWN ORIGIN includes feelings of sadness and emptiness, low energy, and a lack of interest that occurs naturally when experiencing change or stress in life.
Unlike the feelings of sadness and moodiness that are part of everyday life, many people are often unable to deal with their feelings of sadness and moodiness and their feelings last much longer. The mood is accompanied by feelings of irritability and hostility, a growing sense of fatigue, and a sense of hopelessness about the future.

Introduction

Sources of Serious Mood Inconsistencies

Where do disturbances in mood originate? Why do some teens experience changes in mood and moodiness, while others do not? That is not an easy question to answer. Because mood inconsistencies are very complex in nature, they usually do not originate from one source. Rather, many things can lead to mood disturbances in teens, and often it is not only one of the following sources, but a combination of several sources.

Negative Thinking
Distorted, maladaptive, and irrational thinking can cause and enhance feelings of sadness and moodiness. A thorough examination should be conducted by a medical professional to assess teens' thought processes as they relate to and affect feelings.

Genetics and Biology
Family history can influence one's predisposition to moodiness. Similarly, changes in teens' bodies including fluctuating hormones associated with puberty can be a factor. A complete medical and psychological history should be collected by a medical professional to identify family members who may also have experienced mood fluctuations.

Uncontrollable Situations
Situations in which people find themselves unable to control outcomes can enhance feelings of anxiety, sadness, a loss of interest, and a sense of hopelessness and helplessness. An examination of the situations in which teens experience feelings of moodiness should be conducted by a medical professional.

Life Events
An inability to cope with major stressors can be a factor in moodiness. Some of the major stressors that often precede mood disturbances include being bullied, peer pressure, traumatic shock, abuse, differences in sexual orientation, loss of family members, and problems at school. An examination of the life events that may be causing sadness and moodiness should be conducted by a medical professional.

Medical Conditions
Teens who have medical conditions often experience mood disturbances as a secondary symptom. Physical symptoms such as aches and pains should be explored. A teen's medical history can reveal conditions that might induce a mood problem and should be examined by a medical professional.

Substances
Teens often experience mood problems from experimental or chronic use of alcohol and drugs. An examination of a teen's drug and alcohol use should be examined by a medical professional.

Lack of Social Support
Teens who have access to a social support system are much less likely to experience severe and extended bouts of sadness. An examination of a teen's support system should be conducted by a medical professional.

Managing Moods Workbook for Teens Can Help Everyone Who is Moody

The assessments and activities in this workbook are designed to provide facilitators with a wide variety of tools to use in helping people manage their moods. Many choices for self-exploration are provided for facilitators to determine which tools best suit the unique needs of their teens.

The purpose of this workbook is to provide a user-friendly guide to short-term assessments and activities designed to help people conquer feelings of moodiness and experience a greater sense of wellbeing. In addition, this workbook is designed to help provide facilitators and teens with tools and information needed to be aware of mood issues, and overcome the stigma attached to mood issues, NOT to diagnose mood disorders.

In order to help teens successfully deal with moodiness, it is extremely helpful for facilitators to have a variety of appealing, user-friendly assessments and activities to help teens "open-up" and begin to feel as if their moods are less intense and more balanced, and that they are not alone. The *Managing Moods Workbook* for *Teens* provides assessments and self-guided activities to help teens reduce the intensity of moodiness and begin living more effective and fulfilling lives.

When to Worry?

Disturbances in mood are much more painful and numbing than the everyday blues and sadness that most people experience from time to time. These disturbances are much more than a temporary feeling of being down in the dumps, disappointed, sad after a loss, irritable, angry or frustrated. Ongoing, constant moodiness is a pervasive sense of emptiness in which people are unable to engage with daily life. They feel lethargic about everyone and everything, experience a series of highs and lows, and are immobilized to the level that getting out of bed can feel like a difficult task. The good news is that people can develop the cognitive, affective, and behavioral skills needed to decrease the amount, depth and duration of their moodiness and begin to feel a sense of joy, contentment, and wellbeing. **Teens who experience these feelings for an extended period of time are at risk of having a serious mood disturbance and need to seek professional medical and psychological assistance.**

Suicide Warning!

Teens who experience severe bouts of moodiness are often at risk for suicide. Sometimes their feelings can be so strong that they think the only way to escape the pain is to die by suicide. Remember to take any talk about suicide or suicidal acts very seriously. Anyone showing any of the following symptoms needs to be taken seriously, and facilitators can take an active role in their finding help immediately:

- Withdrawing from family, friends, and activities of interest in the past
- Increasing use of harmful substances
- Giving away possessions
- Expressing severe hopelessness about the future
- Making a plan for dying by suicide
- Calling or visiting people to say goodbye
- Preoccupation with death
- Engaging in reckless behavior
- Talking about killing or harming self
- Expressing feelings of being trapped with no way out
- Purchasing or borrowing a weapon

Teens need to do much more than complete the assessments, activities and exercises contained in this workbook if they have serious mental issues. All mood disturbances need to be thoroughly evaluated by a medical professional, and then treated with an appropriate combination of medication and group and/or individual therapy.

Introduction

Format of the *Managing Moods Workbook for Teens*

The *Managing Moods Workbook for Teens* is designed to be used either independently or as part of an established mental health program. You may administer any of the assessments and the guided self-exploration activities to an individual or a group with whom you are working. You may administer any of the assessments and activities over one or more days. Feel free to pick and choose those that best fit the outcomes you desire. The purpose of this workbook is to provide facilitators who work with individuals and groups with a series of reproducible activities that can be used to supplement their work with teens. Because the activity pages in this workbook are reproducible, they can be photocopied as is, or by changes may be made with white out, or by adding additional words to a master to suit each individual or group, and then photocopied.

Assessments

Assessments, with scales for each module, establish a behavioral baseline from which facilitators and teens can gauge progress toward identified goals. This workbook will supplement a facilitator's work by providing assessments designed to measure behavioral baselines for assessing client change. In order to do so, assessments with scoring directions and interpretation materials begin each module. The authors recommend that you begin presenting each topic by asking teens to complete the assessment. Facilitators can choose one or more, or all of the activities relevant to their teens' specific needs and concerns.

The awareness modules contained in this workbook will prompt insight and behavioral change and begin with a scale for the following purposes:
- Help facilitators to develop a numerical baseline of behavior, attitude, and personality characteristics before they begin their plan of treatment.
- Help facilitators gather valuable information about their teen clients/students.
- Help facilitators measure change over time.
- Help teens feel part of the treatment-planning process.
- Provide teens with a starting point to begin to learn more about themselves and their strengths and limitations.
- Facilitators use as pre-tests and post-tests to measure changes in behavior, attitude and personality.
- Facilitators identify patterns that are negatively affecting a teen.

Assessments are a great aid in developing plans for effective change and decreased moodiness.
Be aware of the following when administering, scoring, and interpreting the assessments contained in this workbook:

- The purpose of these assessments is not to pigeonhole or diagnose people, but to allow them to explore various elements of themselves and their situations.
- This workbook contains *self-assessments* and not *tests*. Traditional tests measure knowledge or right or wrong responses. For the assessments provided in this workbook, remind teens that there are no right or wrong answers. These assessments ask only for opinions or attitudes.
- Assessments in this workbook have face value, but have not been formally normed for validity and reliability.
- Assessments in this workbook are based on self-reported data. In other words, the accuracy and usefulness of the information is dependent on the information that teens honestly provide about themselves. Assure them that if they don't want anyone else to know what they wrote, they do not need to share their information. They can be honest.
- Assessments are exploratory exercises and not a judgment of who the teens are as human beings.
- Assessments are not a substitute for professional assistance and/or diagnosis. If you feel any of your teens need more assistance than you can provide, refer them to an appropriate professional.

(Format continued on the next page)

Format of the Managing Moods Workbook for Teens *(continued)*

Assessment Script

When administering the assessments contained in this workbook, please remember that the assessments can be administered, scored, and interpreted by the client/student. If working in a group, facilitator can circulate among teens as they complete assessments to ensure that there are no questions. If working with an individual client/student, facilitators can use the instruction collaboratively. **Please note: As your teens begin the assessments in this workbook, the instructions below are meant to be a guide, so please do not feel you must read them word for word.**

Tell your teens: *"You will be completing a quick assessment related to the topics we are discussing. Assessments are powerful tools, but only if you are honest with yourself. Take your time and be truthful in your responses so that your results are an honest reflection of you. Your level of commitment in completing the assessment truthfully will determine how much you learn about yourself. You do not need to share them with anyone if you don't want to."*

Allow teens to turn to the first page of their assessment and read the instructions silently to themselves. Then tell them: *"All of the assessments have similar formats, but they have different scales, responses, scoring instructions and methods for interpretation. If you do not understand how to complete the assessment, ask me before you turn the page to begin."*

Then tell them: *"There is no time limit for completing the assessments, take your time and work at your own pace. Do not answer the assessments as you think others would like you to answer them or how you think others see you. These assessments are for you to reflect on your life and explore some of the barriers that are keeping you from living a more satisfying life. Before completing each assessment, be sure to read the instructions."*

Make sure that nobody has a question. Then tell them: *"Learning about yourself can be a positive and motivating experience. Don't stress about taking the assessments or discovering your results. Just respond honestly and learn as much about yourself as you can."*

Tell teens to turn the page and begin answering with Question 1. Allow sufficient time for all teens to complete their assessment. Answer any questions people have. It is extremely helpful for you, as the facilitator, to read and/or complete the assessment prior to distributing to the teens. As people begin to finish, read through the instructions for scoring the assessment. Have teens begin to score their assessments and transfer their scores for interpretation. Check to be sure that no one has a question about the scoring.

Review the purpose of the interpretation table included after each assessment. Tell the teens: *"Remember, this assessment was not designed to label you. Rather, it was designed to develop a baseline of your behaviors, to give you a view of where you are, at this time. Regardless of how you score on an assessment, consider it a starting point upon which you can develop healthier habits. Take your time, reflect on your results, and note how they compare to what you already know about yourself."*

After teens have completed, scored, and interpreted their assessment, facilitators can use the self-exploration activities included in each module to supplement their traditional tools and techniques to help teens function more effectively.

(Format continued on the next page)

Format of the Managing Moods Workbook for Teens *(continued)*

Self-Exploration Activities

This workbook will provide self-exploration activities that can be used to induce behavioral change, enhance thinking skills and decrease feelings of sadness and moodiness. These activities, included after each of the assessments, will prompt self-reflection and promote self-understanding. They use a variety of formats to accommodate all learning styles and foster introspection and promote pro-social behaviors, life skills and coping skills. The activities in each module correlate to the assessments to enable you to identify and select activities quickly and easily.

Self-exploration activities assist teens in self-reflection, enhance self-knowledge, identify potential ineffective behaviors, and teach more effective ways of coping with moodiness. They are designed to help teens make a series of discoveries that lead to increased social and emotional competencies, as well as to serve as an energizing way to help teens grow personally and scholastically. These brief, easy-to-use self-reflection tools are designed to promote insight and self-growth.

Many different types of guided self-exploration activities are provided for you to pick and choose the activities that are most needed by your teens and the ones that will be most appealing to them. The unique features of the exploration activities make them user-friendly and appropriate for a variety of individual sessions and group sessions.

In some activities, teens will have opportunities to …

- explore how they could make changes in their lives to feel better. These activities are designed to help teens reflect on their current life situations, discover new ways of living more effectively, and implement changes in their lives to accommodate these skills.

- journal as a way of enhancing their self-awareness. Through journaling prompts, teens will be able to write about the thoughts, attitudes, feelings, and behaviors that have contributed to, or are currently contributing to, their current life situation. Through journaling, teens are able to safely address their concerns, hopes and dreams for the future.

- explore their moodiness issues by examining past behavior for negative patterns and learning new ways of dealing more effectively in the future. These activities are designed to help teens reflect on their lives in ways that will allow them to develop healthier lifestyles.

The facilitator has the choice of how to process the activities – individually, in a full group or with volunteers sharing, etc.

IMPORTANT INFORMATION FOR FACILITATORS
When Using the *Managing Moods Workbook for Teens*

Our goal for this workbook is NOT to diagnose a mental illness, or even for the facilitator to make that diagnosis from this book's content. Our goal is to *touch* on some of the symptoms and possibilities, create realizations, and provide coping methods which will help people to go forward and perhaps consider the possibility of the need for consideration of medications and therapy. It is also to help teens recognize that other people have the same issues, that no shame is connected to them, and mental illness of any degree is not to be stigmatized nor should anyone need to feel like a victim to stereotyping. In this workbook, we are using the phrase *mental condition* in order to include ALL types of mood problems, from just being moody to serious mental illness.

CONFIDENTIALITY: Instruct teens to use NAME CODES when writing or speaking about anyone. Teens completing the activities in this workbook might be asked to respond to assessment items and journal about relationships. Before you begin using the materials in this workbook explain to teens that confidentiality is a term for any action that preserves the privacy of other people. Maintaining confidentiality is extremely important as it shows respect for others and allows – even encourages - teens to explore their feelings without hurting anyone's feelings or fearing gossip, harm or retribution.

In order to maintain this confidentiality, ask teens to assign a NAME CODE for each person they write about as they complete the various activities in the workbook. For example, a friend named **Joey** who **enjoys going to hockey games** might be titled **JLHG** (Joey Loves Hockey Games) for a particular exercise. In order to protect their friends' identities, they will not use people's actual names or initials, just NAME CODES.

Our thanks to these professionals who make us look good!

Art Director – Joy Dey
Editor and Lifelong Teacher – Eileen Regen
Editorial Director – Carlene Sippola
Proofreader Extraordinaire – Jay Leutenberg
Reviewer – Carol Butler
Teen Reviewer – Hannah Lavoie

Special thanks to Sarah L. Ashford
Sarah recognized the need to develop skills towards her own mood management at the age of 16.
She currently studies neuroscience and psychology at The University of Arizona
and advocates for those facing mood challenges.

Our thanks to Dr. Mel Gallen and Dr. Raymond K. Lederman
for helping us launch our new series,
Erasing the Stigma of Mental Illness through Awareness,
of serious, vitally important, yet delicate topics!

Introduction

The Stigma Awareness Approach

Facilitators must keep an open mind about mental health issues and the stigma attached to people experiencing these issues. Rather than thinking of people as having a mental disorder, or being mentally ill, this series, *Erasing the Stigma of Mental Health Issues through Awareness* is designed to help facilitators diminish the stigma that affects people suffering from moodiness. Stigmas occur when people are unduly labeled, and this sets the stage for discrimination and humiliation. Facilitators are able to help erase the stigma of mental health issues through enhanced awareness of the factors that activate the issues. They can accentuate the depth of the problems, and accelerate awareness and understanding.

To assist you, a module entitled **"Erasing the Stigma of Mental Health Issues"** is included to provide activities for helping to erase the stigma associated with mood inconsistencies.

The Awareness Modules

The reproducible awareness exercises contained in this workbook are divided into five modules to help you identify and select assessments and activities easily and quickly:

Module I: How Moody Are You?
This section will help teens identify the depth of their moodiness and identify ways to decrease the intensity of this moodiness.

Module II: Effects of Moodiness
This section will help teens identify the ways that moodiness is affecting their health, relationships, work and social activities.

Module III: Mood Triggers
This section will help teens identify the ways that they experience moodiness in their lives through feelings, thoughts, and behaviors.

Module IV: Roller Coaster Moods
This section will help teens identify the effects of mood instabilities in their lives.

Module V: Erasing the Stigma of Mental Health Issues
This section will help teens explore the stigma of moodiness in their lives and the impact that the stigma has on them.

Table of Contents

MODULE I – How Moody Are You? 15

- How Moody Are You? Introduction and Directions 17
- How Moody Are You? Scale 18
- Scoring Directions 19
- Profile Interpretation 19
- WARNING 19
- Thinking About Your Own Thinking 20
- Converting Negative to Positive Thinking 21
- Changes in My Routine 22
- Reducing Stress 23
- Causes of Moodiness 24–25
- Irritability 26
- Empowerment vs. Helplessness 27
- Optimism vs. Hopelessness 28
- My Feelings 29–30
- Building Resilience 31
- Hiding and Mirroring Emotions 32
- Just Do It! 33
- Feeling Moody 34
- A Letter to Me 35
- To Understand Me 36

MODULE II - Effects of Moodiness 37

- Effects of Moodiness Introduction and Directions 39
- Effects of Moodiness Scale 40–41
- Scoring Directions 42
- Profile Interpretation 42
- Scale Descriptions 42
- Talk to a Trusted Adult 43
- Involving Family and Friends 44
- Positive Thinking = Positive Feelings 45
- My Personal Health 46
- My Healthy Self 47–48
- Let's Get Physical 49
- Relationships 50
- The Impact on My Relationships 51
- Moodiness at School 52
- Managing My Moodiness at School 53
- Social Activities 54

Table of Contents

Get Involved Socially 55
Activating Events 56
My Risky Behaviors 57
Why I Engage in Risky Behaviors 58
Positive Activities 59
My Risky Behavior Contract 60
I Have Choices 61

MODULE III - Mood Triggers 63

Mood Triggers Scale Introduction and Directions 65
Mood Triggers Scale 66–67
Scoring Directions 68
Profile Interpretation 68
Scale Descriptions 68
My Mood Pattern 69
Early Warning Signs 70–71
I'm Overwhelmed and Stressed 72
Reduce Moodiness with Exercise 73
You Are What You Eat 74
Relaxation Techniques 75
That's Funny 76
My Reactions When I'm Moody 77
My Internal Triggers 78
Victim Thinking 79
Worry, Worry, Worry 80
Feeling Good About Myself 81–82

MODULE IV – Roller Coaster Moods 83

Roller Coaster Moods Scale Introduction and Directions 85
Roller Coaster Moods Scale 86
Scoring Directions 87
Profile Interpretation 87
Scale Descriptions 87
Over Excited? Frantic? Frenzied? Agitated? 88
Recognizing Symptoms 89–90
Major Life Decisions 91
To Take or Not To Take? 92
Outlets for Excessive Energy 93
Damage-Repair 94

Table of Contents

My WEEKLY Mood Chart 95
My DAILY Mood Chart 96
Potential Support Network 97
My Impulsive Up-Side Behaviors 98
My Social Rhythms - Weekdays 99
My Social Rhythms - Weekends 100
Activity vs. Inactivity 101
Predictable and Unpredictable Changes 102
Listening 103

MODULE V – Erasing the Stigma of Mental Health Issues 103

Introduction 107
Two Types of Mental Health Stigma 108
The Stigma of Being Known as "Moody" – THE PAST 109
The Stigma of Being Known as "Moody" – THE PRESENT 110
What Animal are YOU? 111
If We Stamp Out the Stigma 112
Glenn Close said... 113
Effects of the Stigma of Moodiness 114
The Stigma of Going to a Mental Health Therapist 115
Stereotypes 116
Coping with the Stigma of Moodiness 117
What Can YOU Do? 118
My Negative Thoughts 119
Focus on Your Strengths 120
Ways I Try to Minimize My Moodiness 121
Ways I am Treated 122
Stay Active 123
Self-Doubt 124
A Poster About the Stigma of Moodiness 125
A Poster About Acceptance of People With Moodiness 126
DE-STIGMA-TIZE with the Facts 127
Coping with the Stigma of a Mental Health Issue 128
Speak Out Against Stigma 129

MODULE I

How Moody Are You?

Nothing lifts me out of a bad mood better than a hard workout on my treadmill. It never fails. To us, exercise is nothing short of a miracle.

~ Cher

Name _____

Date _____

How Moody Are You? Scale
Introduction and Directions

As a teen, you will find that you become moody from time to time. When your moodiness affects and interferes with your effectiveness in school and in your relationships with family and friends, it's good to explore how moody you really are.

You can use the following scale to explore how moody you are in your daily life.

Moodiness brings forth a wide range of emotions. This assessment contains 25 statements related to your level of moodiness. Read each of the statements and decide how much the statement describes you.

- If the statement describes you a lot, circle the number under that column next to that item.
- If the statement describes you sometimes, circle the number under that column next to that item.
- If the statement describes you only a little or not at all, circle the number under that column next to that item.

In the following example, the circled number under "A Lot" indicates the statement is descriptive of the person completing the inventory a lot of the time.

	A LOT	SOMETIMES	A LITTLE/NONE
I have sleep difficulty – either I have trouble sleeping or I sleep too much	(3)	2	1

This is not a test. Since there are no right or wrong answers, do not spend too much time thinking about your answers. Be sure to respond to every statement.

Turn to the next page and begin.

Managing Moods Workbook for Teens

How Moody Are You? Scale

	A LOT	SOMETIMES	A LITTLE/NONE
I have sleep difficulty – either I have trouble sleeping or I sleep too much	3	2	1
I have quick swings in mood from glad to sad	3	2	1
I have appetite problems – either I have no appetite or I can't stop eating	3	2	1
I am irritable around others	3	2	1
I am more aggressive than usual	3	2	1
I feel fatigued and sluggish	3	2	1
I do not share information about my moodiness with family	3	2	1
I tend to have a negative attitude	3	2	1
I am preoccupied with death	3	2	1
I engage in reckless, risky behavior	3	2	1
I don't want people to know how I am feeling	3	2	1
I have lost interest in being with my friends	3	2	1
I feel *empty*	3	2	1
I cannot make good decisions	3	2	1
I feel as if my life is hopeless	3	2	1
I think about suicide	3	2	1
I judge myself harshly	3	2	1
I feel embarrassed after I am moody	3	2	1
I get angry easily	3	2	1
I find myself picking fights with others	3	2	1
I cry more often than I want to	3	2	1
I feel agitated	3	2	1
I find it hard to concentrate in school	3	2	1
I can't seem to "get going"	3	2	1
Even if asked, I will not talk to people about my moods	3	2	1

TOTAL = _____

Go to the Scoring Directions on the next page

How Moody Are You? Scale
Scoring Directions

Moodiness can interfere with relationships, work, school, social activities, and participation in the community.

The How Moody Are You? Scale is designed to help you explore how persistent your feelings of moodiness are and how disruptive your moods are in your daily life. For the scale you just completed, add the numbers that you circled. This score will give you some sense of how moody you are. Your total will range from 25 to 75.

Then, transfer this total to the space below:

Level of Moodiness Total   =   _____

Profile Interpretation

Individual Scale Score	Result	Indications
25–28	Low	Low scores indicate a low level of moodiness. Complete the following exercises to ensure you reduce your moody feelings even further.
29–32	Moderate	Moderate scores indicate a medium high level of moodiness. Complete the following exercises to ensure you reduce your moody feelings even further.
33–75	High	High scores indicate a high level of moodiness. Complete the following exercises to ensure you reduce your moody feelings even further.

WARNING

Teens who are experiencing moderate and high levels of moody feelings, thoughts and behaviors can be at risk for suicide. Sometimes moody feelings can be so strong that teens think that the only way to escape the pain is to take their own life. You need to remember that if you are having these feelings, or spend time thinking about how you could take your life, you need to talk to a medical professional and/or call the confidential National Suicide Prevention Hotline, 1-800-273-TALK (8255), anytime, 24/7.

The following activities are designed to help reduce your level of moodiness. Regardless of how you scored on the scale, please complete all of the activities.

Managing Moods Workbook for Teens

Thinking About Your Own Thinking

Teens who experience mood disturbances often engage in negative thinking.
EVERYONE has negative thoughts and there are many different methods of negative thinking. Which ones describe your thinking? USE NAME CODES.

Type of Negative Thinking	My Negative Thoughts	How They Make Me Feel and Act
Self-Doubt (Example: I'm not good enough, I am not talented in anything!)		
Pessimism (Example: I'm doomed, Nothing ever works out, etc.)		
Powerlessness (Example: MBJ does not allow me to do what I want to do.)		
Demanding Thinking (Example: I should have, I must, He should have.)		
Negativism (Example: Focusing on the negative in a situation and unable to see or care about the positive side.)		

Which type of thinking do you exhibit most often? How can you be more alert to this type of thinking?

_____

_____

How Moody Are You?

Converting Negative to Positive Thinking

EVERYONE can work to make negative thinking more positive.
Complete the table below based on the negative thoughts you identified. Use NAME CODES.

My Negative Thoughts	More Accurate Positive Thoughts	My Affirmation
Example: "I'm not as good as FGM at math."	"I don't need to compare myself to others."	"I try hard and I am good enough just as I am."

Cut out your written "My Affirmation" statements from the third column above and place them in your room, on your door and mirror, by your computer and taped to your laptop — anywhere that you can review them often. If you are comfortable, share them with the group.

Changes in My Routine

One can change routines to feel less moody. These types of changes are often small changes that you can make for yourself to feel better and be less moody. Changes in routine can encompass many different aspects of one's life.

Complete the table below to explore changes that you could make to feel less moody. USE NAME CODES.

Aspects of My Life	Current Routines or Habits	How This Affects Me	How I Can Be More Effective
Example: Relaxation	Watch television before going to bed.	I go to bed stimulated and just can't relax.	Listen to relaxing music before bedtime.
Relaxation			
Exercise			
Sleep			
Nutrition			
Social Support			
Humor			
Other			

The most important affects of moodiness on my daily routine are _____

_____

_____

Reducing Stress

Stress can intensify feelings of depression. Following are some stress-management techniques to use to improve a deflated mood.

Complete this table to identify effective stress-management techniques. USE NAME CODES.

Aspects of My Lifestyle	Tried and Liked It. Why Do You Like It?	Have Not Tried It. Why Haven't You?	Tried and Do Not Like it. Why Not?
Relaxation – Find a quiet place to relax, meditate, do yoga, listen to soothing music, follow some guided imagery, draw, write, breathe deeply.			
Exercise – Plan regular exercise, physical activity like sports, walking, jogging, aerobic exercising, yoga, martial arts.			
Sleep – Before bed, have a nighttime sleep routine: avoid eating, drinking, and physical activity. Make sure the room conditions are comfortable.			
Nutrition – Eat nutritional well-balanced meals, which enhances your ability to fight moodiness.			
Social Support – Confide in and talk with trusted friends and family about your moodiness.			
Humor – Tell and enjoy appropriate jokes, relay funny stories to others, watch humorous television shows or movies.			
Other			

Managing Moods Workbook for Teens

Causes of Moodiness

Moodiness develops from a variety of causes. By becoming more aware of some of the causes of depressed moods, you can develop a plan to overcome them. For each of the following items in the next two pages, place an X over the spot on the line that you think describes your level of mood alterations. USE NAME CODES.

                                        Sunny   Gloomy

Loneliness   0---------------------------5---------------------------10

Explain _____

_____

                                        Sunny   Gloomy

Lack of social support   0---------------------------5---------------------------10

Explain _____

_____

                                        Sunny   Gloomy

Recent stressful life experiences   0---------------------------5---------------------------10

Explain _____

_____

                                        Sunny   Gloomy

Family history of depression   0---------------------------5---------------------------10

Explain _____

_____

                                        Sunny   Gloomy

Friendship or relationship problems 0---------------------------5---------------------------10

Explain _____

_____

                                        Sunny   Gloomy

Low self-esteem   0---------------------------5---------------------------10

Explain _____

_____

(Continued on the next page)

Causes of Moodiness *(Continued)*

Problems at home

Sunny 0---------------------------5---------------------------10 Gloomy

Explain _____

_____

Trauma or abuse

Sunny 0---------------------------5---------------------------10 Gloomy

Explain _____

_____

Alcohol or drug abuse

Sunny 0---------------------------5---------------------------10 Gloomy

Explain _____

_____

Problems in school

Sunny 0---------------------------5---------------------------10 Gloomy

Explain _____

_____

Being bullied

Sunny 0---------------------------5---------------------------10 Gloomy

Explain _____

_____

Loss of loved one(s)

Sunny 0---------------------------5---------------------------10 Gloomy

Explain _____

_____

Other

Sunny 0---------------------------5---------------------------10 Gloomy

Explain _____

_____

Irritability

Irritability is demonstrated through being hostile or grumpy, or having the inability to control one's temper. For many teens, a major sign of moodiness presents itself as irritability.

How do you show your irritability?

Describe a situation or time when you were quite irritable. USE NAME CODES.

_____
_____
_____
_____
_____

Who was around? _____

How did you behave? How did the other person/people react?

_____
_____
_____
_____

How did you then react?

_____
_____
_____
_____

When you felt yourself being irritable, either at first or thinking about the instance later, how could you have better controlled or handled it?

_____
_____
_____
_____

Empowerment vs. Helplessness

People feel helpless when they are unable to make a situation better. People feel empowered when they feel they can significantly affect their situations.

In the table below discuss the ways you feel helpless in four major areas of your life: family, school, friends and dating relationships and how you can become more empowered. USE NAME CODES.

Areas of My Life	How I Feel Helpless	How I Could Feel More Empowered
Family		
School		
Friends		
Dating Relationships		
Other		

What is the most important change you can make? _____

_____

_____

Optimism vs. Hopelessness

People often feel hopeless about their situations and/or the way their life seems to be going. They feel optimistic and empowered when they feel they are in control.

In the table below discuss ways you feel hopeless in four major areas of your life: family, school, friends and in dating relationships. USE NAME CODES.

Areas of My Life	How I Feel Hopeless	How I Can Feel More Empowered
Family		
School		
Friends		
Dating Relationships		
Other		

What is the most important change you can make? _____

How Moody Are You?

My Feelings

Complete these prompts to assist you in exploring your feelings and the extent of your moodiness. If any of the following are not issues for you, write "not my issue" and explain why.

My persistent sad mood _____

My persistent anxious mood _____

My persistent *empty* mood _____

My sudden swings in mood _____

My feelings of hopelessness _____

My feelings of helplessness _____

My feelings of guilt _____

My feelings of lack of self-worth _____

My loss of interest or pleasure in activities that I once enjoyed _____

My changes in energy level _____

(Continued on the next page)

My Feelings *(Continued)*

My difficulty concentrating _____

My difficulty remembering _____

My difficulty making decisions _____

My changes in sleep patterns _____

My eating issues _____

My thoughts of death or suicide _____

My thoughts of hurting someone _____

My restlessness _____

My irritability _____

My changes in thinking _____

My risk-taking behavior _____

My _____

How Moody Are You?

Building Resilience

Resiliency is the ability to bounce back. Resilient people can adapt in the face of adversity, trauma, loss and many other forms of stress. They are able to bounce back after tragedies such as hurricanes, war, loss of job or loved ones. When teens are able to deal with any type of negative events and changes in their lives, they are said to be resilient.

Journal about each of these ways to build resiliency, and how you will accomplish each one.
USE NAME CODES.

I will make more connections by _____

_____

_____

I will identify the types of events that cause me the most stress. These events are _____

_____

_____

I will try to be more hopeful by _____

_____

_____

I will develop some short-term personal or academic goals to achieve including _____

_____

_____

I will find ways to learn more about myself by _____

_____

_____

I will take care of myself better by _____

_____

_____

Do you have a role model of someone who is resilient? Share with the group.

Hiding and Mirroring Emotions

What do you see when you look in the mirror? Often times what we see is an illusion and not reality because one hides emotions from others. Here are two "mirrors" below.

Pretend you are looking in the mirror on the left.
   Draw a picture of how others see you.

Now move to the second mirror on the right.
   Draw a picture or a collage of words that describe how you see yourself.

HOW OTHERS SEE ME	HOW I SEE MYSELF

What are the differences in the two mirrors? _____
_____
_____

How Moody Are You?

Just Do It!

When teens feel sad, they often shy away from people and activities. They want to wait until these feelings pass to get back to normal interactions and daily activities. This often leads to a continued downward spiral. It is better for them to encourage and motivate themselves to be with other people and continue engaging in fun, safe activities.

In the spaces that follow, write about or draw two people you stop interacting with when you are moody, and do the same to show two fun activities you stop doing when you feel *down*.

PERSON 1	PERSON 2
ACTIVITY 1	**ACTIVITY 2**

How can you make a promise to yourself to do at least one of these fun, safe activities when you feel like isolating or withdrawing? _____

Managing Moods Workbook for Teens

Feeling Moody

It helps to identify how we appear to others, and how we behave, when we are moody. To begin, circle the "moody" words in the word search. HINT: The 2-word "Search Words" have a letter between them.

A	S	D	F	G	U	N	R	E	A	C	H	A	B	L	E	H	J	K	L
Z	X	C	V	B	N	M	Q	W	M	I	S	E	R	A	B	L	E	E	S
G	R	M	P	T	Y	U	I	S	A	D	O	P	M	N	B	V	C	A	T
R	E	L	O	K	J	H	A	U	H	G	F	D	S	A	O	I	U	U	R
O	Y	T	U	P	R	E	W	L	Z	C	A	S	N	O	T	B	I	N	E
U	C	A	T	P	E	T	U	L	A	N	T	U	M	B	E	C	R	A	S
C	S	X	Y	U	S	E	V	E	I	L	L	E	H	U	M	O	R	P	S
H	A	N	X	I	O	U	S	N	S	T	E	K	R	L	P	E	I	P	E
Y	D	U	T	E	B	B	G	E	R	G	J	I	O	H	E	N	T	R	D
L	A	I	P	T	W	A	B	L	K	A	S	D	T	H	R	Y	A	O	N
M	G	L	F	R	O	W	N	Y	O	U	R	I	E	Y	A	E	B	A	L
T	L	T	A	A	R	N	D	N	O	O	E	R	M	A	M	A	L	C	O
N	U	L	Y	N	T	N	B	A	D	E	M	O	O	D	E	M	E	H	N
Y	M	B	R	O	H	S	D	K	Y	A	N	Y	D	J	N	A	C	K	G
Y	U	O	L	I	L	S	H	S	U	L	K	S	O	P	T	H	I	B	A
A	N	G	R	Y	E	A	I	R	L	E	L	E	A	N	A	D	J	L	F
E	Y	N	N	O	S	M	A	S	U	N	S	T	O	B	L	E	N	E	A
K	B	O	R	P	S	L	A	Y	S	C	E	H	S	S	A	S	P	E	C
A	K	S	C	H	I	E	N	E	S	E	J	Y	G	O	S	E	T	O	E
T	H	C	R	O	S	S	E	W	O	O	G	R	U	M	P	Y	D	W	R

Think about times when you are moody.
Check your "top 10" of how you are feeling at those times when you are moody.
Then, check your "top 10" of how you think you appear to others at those moody times.

Search Words	How I Feel	How I Appear to Others
Angry		
Anxious		
Bad mood		
Cross		
Frowny		
Gloomy		
Glum		
Grouchy		
Grumpy		
Ill humor		
Long face		
Miserable		

Search Words	How I Feel	How I Appear to Others
Mope		
Morose		
Petulant		
Pouty		
Stressed		
Sulk		
Sullen		
Temperamental		
Unapproachable		
Unreachable		
Unstable		
Worthless		

A Letter to Me

It is helpful to think towards the future and project who you want to be.

Write a letter from the *current you* to the *future you*, fifteen years from now.
What good advice do you have for the *future you*?
What do you want to see in yourself (characteristics, habits, hobbies, relationships, etc.)?

Dear _____,

_____

_____

_____

_____

_____

_____

_____

_____

_____

_____

_____

_____

_____

_____

_____

_____

_____

Sincerely, _____

If you are comfortable, read your letter to the group.

Put the letter in an envelope and write "To be opened _____." Save it!
(DATE 15 YEARS LATER)

"To Understand Me..."

> *To understand me, you have to meet me and be around me.*
> *And then, only if I'm in a good mood — don't meet me in a bad mood.*
>
> ~ Avril Lavigne

What does this quote mean to you?

_____
_____
_____

How do people relate to you when you are in a good mood?

_____
_____
_____

How do you relate to yourself when you are in a good mood?

_____
_____
_____

How do people relate to you when you are in a bad mood?

_____
_____
_____

How do you relate to yourself when you are in a bad mood?

_____
_____
_____

When you're in a bad mood, what can you say to let others know how you are feeling, to help them understand?

_____
_____
_____

Remember that you have many options for coping with your moodiness, and you do not have to suffer alone. Many people are around you to support you in helpful, healthy ways in your efforts to overcome your moodiness. You just need to let them.

MODULE II
Effects of Moodiness

My best personality trait [is] that I think I'm very approachable. My worst is that I can be moody.

~ Enrique Iglesias

Name _____

Date _____

Effects of Moodiness Scale
Introduction and Directions

Teens in general are not aware of their moodiness and the effects that this moodiness has on their life. Therefore it is important for you to develop awareness of the symptoms of moodiness in four major areas of your life:

- Health
- Feelings
- School
- Behaviors

This assessment contains 32 statements designed to help you explore how your moodiness may be affecting each life area. Read each of the statements and decide the statement that describes you. If the statement does describe you, circle the number in the YES column next to that item.
If the statement does not describe you, circle the number in the NO column next to that item.

In the following example, the circled 1 indicates the statement does not describe the person completing the inventory:

Often, in my everyday life …	YES	NO
I am unusually tired	2	(1)

This is not a test. Since there are no right or wrong answers, do not spend too much time thinking about your answers. Be sure to respond to every statement.

Turn to the next page and begin.

Effects of Moodiness Scale

	YES	NO
Often, in my everyday life…		
I am unusually tired	2	1
I have headaches	2	1
I have a huge appetite – or – I have no appetite	2	1
I stay awake at night or sleep too much during the day	2	1
I often have stomachaches	2	1
I feel pain for no reason	2	1
I feel extremely stressed	2	1
I have no energy	2	1

H   TOTAL = _____

Often, related to my feelings…

	YES	NO
I feel gloomy	2	1
I feel worthless or just "wrong"	2	1
I don't feel good about myself	2	1
I feel isolated	2	1
I feel helpless and not in control	2	1
I feel like crying a lot of the time	2	1
I feel irritable or agitated	2	1
I feel pessimistic about my life	2	1

F   TOTAL = _____

(Continued on the next page)

Effects of Moodiness Scale *(Continued)*

	YES	NO

Often, at school…

I have low energy	2	1
I can't concentrate well	2	1
I am late or miss a lot of days	2	1
I have seen my grades drop	2	1
I feel as if I'm under too much pressure	2	1
I get into arguments or fights a lot	2	1
I can't do my homework or assignments	2	1
I withdraw or overreact when I am criticized	2	1

S   TOTAL = _____

Often, when it comes to my behavior…

I engage in reckless behavior	2	1
I feel more rebellious	2	1
I have become violent	2	1
I have begun to self-mutilate	2	1
I have increased my substance use	2	1
I engage in unsafe sexual activity	2	1
I participate in something illegal	2	1
I have lost interest in activities I have always enjoyed	2	1

B   TOTAL = _____

Go to the Scoring Directions on the next page

Managing Moods Workbook for Teens

Effects of Moodiness Scale Scoring Directions

The assessment you just completed is designed to measure the effects of moodiness on various aspects of your life. For each of the sections on the previous pages, count the scores you circled. Put that total on the line marked TOTAL at the end of each section.

Then, transfer your total to the space below:

H = HEALTH TOTAL _____

F = FEELINGS TOTAL _____

S = SCHOOL TOTAL _____

B = BEHAVIOR TOTAL _____

Add your four scores together for your GRAND TOTAL. _____

Profile Interpretation

Individual Scale Score	Grand Total	Result	Indications
8 – 9	32 – 37	Low	Low scores indicate that you are not being affected too much by your moodiness. Complete the following exercises to reduce the effects even more.
10 – 14	38 – 57	Moderate	Moderate scores indicate that you are being somewhat affected by your moodiness. Complete the following exercises to reduce the effects.
15 – 16	58 – 64	High	High scores indicate that you are being greatly affected by your moodiness. Complete the following exercises to reduce the effects even more.

Individual Scale Descriptions

HEALTH – People scoring high on this scale tend to feel the effect of moodiness on their personal health. They have limited energy, issues with eating, and may even have trouble sleeping.

FEELINGS – People scoring high on this scale tend to feel the effects of moodiness through their feelings. They feel isolated, gloomy, and helpless to make significant changes in their life. They may feel agitated and pessimistic. They may want to cry a lot of the time.

SCHOOL – People scoring high on this scale tend to feel the effect of moodiness on their ability to function in school, complete homework assignments, and relate positively to teachers and peers at school.

BEHAVIOR – People scoring high on this scale tend to feel the effect of moodiness in their behaviors. They may be engaging in various types of reckless behavior, or even violent behavior. They may lose interest in activities in which they had past interest, and may begin to get into trouble.

GRAND TOTAL – High scores on all four scales indicate that the person is affected greatly by moodiness. The following pages will be helpful to everyone, no matter how they scored.

Effects of Moodiness

Talk to a Trusted Adult

When teens are moody, they may think that some of the adults in their life will not understand their situation. Although that may be true of some of the adults in their life, there are trusted adults who want to see them do well, are willing to listen and will understand. Identify these people with whom you are able to trust in the table below.

If you do not feel you can completely trust any of the adults in your life, identify people in the table below whom you can possibly trust, why, and how this people can help you. Then, try to get to know them better to decide if you can trust them.

Who?	Trusted Adults NAME CODES	Why I Trust This Person	How This Person Can Help Me
Example: Family Members	*MGM*	*He always listens and I know I can confide in him.*	*He can help me find a therapist or counselor.*
Family Members			
Friends			
People in My Community			
People at My Place of Worship			
People at Work			
People at My School			
Other			

Involving Family & Friends

Having the support of trusted family members and trusted friends can be extremely helpful in managing moody feelings. This support might even strengthen relationships.

In the table below, write about the ways that your friends and family can support you. Explain how you could ask for their support. Explain how they can help you.

This Person Can Support Me When I Am Moody	NAME CODES	When and How This Person Can Support Me	How I Can Ask for Support Stating My Needs
Who can be patient?			
Who can be more understanding?			
Who could stop avoiding me?			
Who would allow me to have alone time?			
Who is willing to listen to me?			
Who wants to learn about my mood problems?			
Who will tell me when I am being difficult?			
Other			
Other			
Other			

Positive Thinking = Positive Feelings

*"We either make ourselves miserable or we make ourselves strong.
The amount of work is the same."*

~ Carlos Castaneda

In order to build yourself up vs. break yourself down, you need to convert your negative thinking into more positive thinking. One way to do this is to simply recognize what is happening in your own mind. In this case, attend to the stream of thoughts that go through your head when you are moody.
Here is an example:

- **Negative thoughts in my head:** "Nobody loves me!" "I'll never find someone with whom to share my life."
- **Feelings that follow:** Low self-esteem, loneliness, fear and/or hopelessness.
- **Where is the evidence?** There is probably evidence to the contrary. "I do have people who love me." and "I have plenty of time to meet someone special."
- **How I could form my thoughts differently**: "I am worthy of being loved." "I will find someone if I don't give up." "If I continue engaging in social activities in places where I can meet new people!"

Now that you have the formula for successfully reversing your negative thinking, you try it below:
USE NAME CODES.

Negative Thoughts That Often Run Through My Head	Feelings That Follow	Where is the Evidence?	How I Could Form My Thoughts Differently

With whom do you usually have negative thoughts? Why? What can you do about it?

_____

_____

When and where do you usually have negative thoughts? Why? What can you do about it?

_____

_____

Managing Moods Workbook for Teens

My Personal Health

The effect of moodiness on personal health is not always obvious. Some of the effects are more pronounced than others.

In the table below, identify how you react when you're moody, how this moodiness affects how you feel physically, and what you can do about it. USE NAME CODES.

Lifestyle	How I React When I'm Moody	How I Am Affected	How I Can Cope Better
Example: Food choices	*I eat sweets.*	*I feel sick and get very tired and then gain weight.*	*I could eat other foods that aren't so sugary.*
Food Choices			
Exercise			
Sleep			
Relaxation			
Professional Help			
Spirituality			
Other			

If you are experiencing symptoms of moodiness that are affecting your health, it is time to consult medical help.

Effects of Moodiness

My Healthy Self

People taking care of themselves in a healthy, non-risky way can cope with moodiness more easily than those who do not take care of themselves in this way.

For each of these sentence starters, write how you can manage your moodiness by taking care of yourself in these ways. If any do not apply to you, write *"not my issue"* and explain why.

Example: *I can stop staying up late at night and being too tired in school.*

I can stop _____
_____
_____

I can eat _____
_____
_____

I can exercise _____
_____
_____

I can enjoy _____
_____
_____

I can take time for _____
_____
_____

I can sleep _____
_____
_____

(Continued on the next page)

My Healthy Self *(Continued)*

I can journal my thoughts by _____
_____
_____

I can take time to meditate by _____
_____
_____

I can find professional help by _____
_____
_____

I can stop using _____
_____
_____

I can explore my religious and/or spirituality practices by_____
_____
_____

I can take my medications regularly by _____
_____
_____

I can_____
_____
_____

Effects of Moodiness

Let's Get Physical

Often, teens who experience moodiness stop participating in their favorite physical activities. Physical activity has been shown to greatly reduce the effects of moodiness. Think about the amount of physical activity you participate in each week, how much time you spend, how it makes you feel, and if you don't do it, why not.

Physical Activity	How Much Time Per Week?	How It Makes Me Feel	If I Don't Do It, Why Not?
Exercise			
Ride a bicycle			
Walk, jog and/or walk a pet			
Play sports			
Join a gym			
Engage in aerobic activities			
Lift weights			
Practice yoga, tai chi, etc.			
Aerobics or dance classes			
Swim or Aquatic exercise			
Work around the house			
Take stairs			
Stretch			
Other			
Other			

Go back to the list above and put a check by the activities you are willing to do more regularly.

Managing Moods Workbook for Teens

Relationships

Moodiness often is accompanied by feelings that may be affecting relationships with other important people in one's life.

Below, explore how you believe your moody feelings might be affecting your relationships.
USE NAME CODES.

Relationship	Signs of My Moodiness	How It Affects This Person	How That Makes Me Feel
Family Member Name *LMD NAME CODE*	I "snap" at her when she asks me to do chores around the house.	She feels like I don't respect her.	Ashamed.
Family Member Name_____ Name_____ Name_____ Name_____ Name_____			
Friend Name_____ Name_____ Name_____			
Neighbor Name_____ Name_____			
School Personnel Name_____ Name_____			
Other Name_____			

How important is it to you to change the way your moodiness affects these relationships?
_____

How will you do it?_____
_____

Effects of Moodiness

The Impact on My Relationships

Coping with moodiness can be made easier by being aware of the impact moodiness is having, and then, ideally, figuring out what to do about it.

Below, complete the sentence starters by writing about the impact of your moodiness on your relationships. USE NAME CODES on the blank line in the first part of each sentence, 1 through 6. Respond to the sentences that apply to you and your relationship(s).

1. _____ gets angry at me _____

2. _____ stays away from me _____

3. _____ says it is all in my head _____

4. _____ becomes tired of me and my moodiness _____

5. _____ excludes me from _____

6. _____ doesn't even try to understand me, instead _____

What I can do to improve my moodiness and its impact on my relationships. _____

… Managing Moods Workbook for Teens

Moodiness at School

Moodiness may affect one's performance in school and in relationships with peers and teachers, as well as affecting one's ability to succeed.

Below, identify all of the ways your moodiness is affecting your performance in school.
USE NAME CODES.

Important Aspects of School	How I am Affected	How I Can Do Better
Example: Completing work in class	*I don't have energy and just want to sit there.*	*I could try to get more sleep so I am not so tired.*
Completing work in class		
Ability to focus and pay attention		
Completing work outside of class		
Arriving at school on time		
Relationships with friends		
Relationships with teachers		
Other		
Other		

Effects of Moodiness

Managing My Moodiness at School

Coping with moodiness can be made much easier by taking care of yourself.

TIPS
- Develop good routines for going to bed and getting enough sleep.
- Wake up in plenty of time to have a good breakfast and not feel rushed to complete any unfinished assignments and/or home responsibilities.
- Maintain or become involved in afterschool activities. Do not withdraw from them.
- Prioritize duties and responsibilities.
- Do not overdo and take on more activities than you can easily handle. Finding time to be alone, read, relax, take a walk, etc., is sometimes necessary.
- Break big tasks into small steps to avoid feeling overwhelmed.
- Learn stress-management techniques to deal with pressure.
- Be aware of how your thinking influences how you feel and how you behave.
- Talk with a trusted adult.

Which of the actions will you begin immediately? How will you do so?

_____

_____

_____

Which of your regular activities are important to continue?

_____

_____

_____

Which of your activities would be wise for you to discontinue?

_____

_____

_____

What types of necessary tasks seem overwhelming to you?

_____

_____

_____

How can you break these tasks down into smaller steps so you are not so overwhelmed?

_____

_____

_____

Managing Moods Workbook for Teens

Social Activities

When anyone is feeling moody, the first instinct may be to isolate from others. This is not a good thing to do. When people are by themselves for a long time, they tend to dwell too much on the negative, and also, they can get into trouble. Interacting with other people with a positive attitude can be a tremendous help.

Below, write about some ways you can continue to be involved in healthy, not risky, extra-curricular and social activities. USE NAME CODES.

Social Activities	Social Activities I Enjoy	How They Help Me
Example: Sports-Related	I enjoy watching my friends play soccer.	I see other people I know from school at the games.
Sports-Related		
School-Related		
Family-Related		
Friend-Related		
Healthy, not risky, fun		
Creative		
Cultural		
Religious/Spiritual		
Other		
Other		

What types of activities have you given up because of your changeable moods?

_____

_____

Would you consider resuming any of these activities? _____ When? _____

Effects of Moodiness

Get Involved Socially

Coping with moods can affect one's interest in all daily activities, especially social plans. A common reaction is to withdraw from other people and activities. When one begins to limit social and recreational pursuits, one also begins to shut down physically.

Think about the following sentence starters as they relate to your participation in social and recreational activities. USE NAME CODES.

When I feel moody,

I want to be by myself because _____
_____
_____

I don't feel like being sociable, so I _____
_____
_____

I miss taking part in social and recreational activities such as _____
_____
_____

I feel bad later because I missed out on _____
_____
_____

I worry that I give others the impression that _____
_____
_____

I feel as if I am _____
_____
_____

© 2014 WHOLE PERSON ASSOCIATES, 101 W. 2ND ST., SUITE 203, DULUTH MN 55802 • 800-247-6789

Activating Events

When people feel moody, they often shy away from people and activities. They want to wait until the moodiness passes to return to normal daily activities. This often leads to a continued downward spiral. Their thinking often triggers this downward spiral.

Following is an explanation of how negative thoughts keep people from engaging in social and recreational activities. The good news is that you are able to reverse these negative thoughts and turn them into positive ones.

SOME TACTICS

Identify the activating event – In this case, it is your negative thinking about engaging in social and recreational activities. This technique will work for any activating event in your life. What is an event coming up in which you would like to attend or engage? This could be hanging out with friends, a party, playing video games with a friend, sports events, family vacation, etc.

_____

Identify your negative thoughts – Identify the negative thoughts that occur as a result of your beliefs about taking part in the event you identified above.

_____
_____

Identify the consequences of your negative thinking. What do you do in response to your negative thoughts?

_____
_____

Now you need to dispute those thoughts! Several questions you need to ask yourself:

Where am I finding proof for my thinking?

_____

In what ways could I be jumping to conclusions?

_____

Could I be making a pessimistic prediction of the future? If so, how?

_____

When or how am I giving in to "should statements" (You should stay home because….")?

_____

You can challenge all of your negative thinking with this method!
Save this page and refer to it from time to time.

Effects of Moodiness

My Risky Behaviors

Teens who feel moody often find themselves getting involved in risky behaviors.

Think about the tie between your risky behavior and your moodiness. Below, identify your risky behaviors and how you might avoid these types of behaviors. USE NAME CODES.

My Risky Behaviors	How My Moodiness Is Tied into the Behavior	How I Can Steer Clear of This Risky Behavior
Driving		
An Addiction		
Thoughts of Suicide		
Thoughts or Actions of Harming Others		
Tobacco/Alcohol/ Drug Use		
Emotional, Physical, Sexual or Verbal (Bullying) Abuse		
Unsafe Sex		
Other		
Other		

Which of your risky behaviors do you know you need to eliminate? Why? _____

_____

_____

How will you start? _____

_____

_____

© 2014 WHOLE PERSON ASSOCIATES, 101 W. 2ND ST., SUITE 203, DULUTH MN 55802 • 800-247-6789

Why I Engage in Risky Behaviors

Research shows that teens who engage in one risky behavior are more likely to engage in additional risky behaviors. Teens have a variety of reasons for engaging in risky behavior, and now it is time to explore those reasons.

Complete the table below. First, list your most risky behavior:

Reasons Teens Engage in Risky Behaviors	How My Risky Behavior Is Related to How I Feel	A Safer Behavior That Would Give Me the Same Feeling Is …
Physical changes		
Search for independence		
Peer pressure		
Rebellion		
Need to be "cool"		
Need to be accepted as part of a group		
Need to feel better about myself		
Challenge to experiment		
Other		

What risky behavior do you want to stop immediately? How will you do so?

_____

_____

Effects of Moodiness

Positive Activities

It is important (and possible!) for teens to substitute positive activities instead of risky activities.

In the table below, identify your risky behaviors, more positive activities to engage in, and how the change will help decrease your moodiness. USE NAME CODES.

My Risky Behaviors	Positive Activities to Replace My Risky Behavior	How This Change Can Decrease My Moodiness
Example: I smoke after school with my friends.	*Go for a walk with friends after school. Exercise feels good.*	*The exercise and having time with friends who don't smoke will help.*

Share with others in the room the responses to how your changes can decrease your moodiness.

My Risky Behavior Contract

I agree to stop participating in these risky behaviors: _____

_____

_____

_____

_____

_____

I will replace the above risky behaviors with these healthy behaviors: _____

_____

_____

_____

_____

_____

When I successfully replace risky behaviors with healthy behaviors, I will accomplish . . . _____

_____

_____

_____

_____

_____

When I fail to replace risky behaviors with healthy behaviors, my consequences will be . . . _____

_____

_____

_____

_____

_____

Signed

    Me _____ Date _____

    A trusted adult _____ Date _____

This contract will be reviewed on these dates: _____

I Have Choices

"I have the choice of being constantly active and happy, or introspectively passive and sad. Or, I can go mad by ricocheting in between."

~ Sylvia Plath

What does this quote mean to you?
_____
_____
_____

How did you feel when reading this quote? _____
_____
_____
_____

What is the advantage of being active and distracted? _____
_____
_____
_____

Give an example and the results. _____
_____
_____
_____

What is the disadvantage of being active and distracted? _____
_____
_____
_____

Give an example and the results. _____
_____
_____
_____

If you are willing, share examples with others in the room.

MODULE III
Mood Triggers

*I have seen the sea
when it is stormy and wild;
when it is quiet and serene;
when it is dark and moody.
And in all its moods,
I see myself.*

~ Martin Buxbaum

Name _____

Date _____

Mood Triggers Scale
Introduction and Directions

Teen moodiness can be caused, or triggered, by a variety of external events and internal sources. Some triggers are external like being bullied or losing loved ones, while some are internally motivated like low self-esteem or feelings of hopelessness. By becoming more aware of some of these causes of moodiness, you can feel empowered to develop a plan for overcoming them.

However, sometimes there are no triggers at all – moodiness just happens.

Read each statement carefully and decide if the statement is related to your moodiness or not. If the statement affects your mood **A Lot**, circle the number 3 next to the statement in that column. If it affects your mood **Some**, circle the number 2 next to the statement in that column. If it has **No Effect**, circle the number 1 next to the statement in that column. Pay no attention to the numbers; read only the column headings. Complete all of the items before going back to score the assessment.

In the following example, the circled 2 indicates that the statement has **some** effect on the person completing the scale.

External factors that trigger my moodiness:	A Lot	Some	No Effect
Addiction(s) 3		(2)	1

This is not a test and there are no right or wrong answers. Do not spend too much time thinking about your answers. Your initial response will be the most true for you. Be sure to respond to every statement.

Turn to the next page and begin.

Managing Moods Workbook for Teens

Mood Triggers Scale

Factors that trigger my moodiness:	A Lot	Some	No Effect
Addiction(s)	3	2	1
Lack of emotional support	3	2	1
Effects of having responsibilities	3	2	1
Sexual orientation	3	2	1
Lack of friends	3	2	1
Family history of mental health issues	3	2	1
Increased independence or increased lack of independence	3	2	1
Problems at home	3	2	1
Financial problems	3	2	1
School problems	3	2	1
Being hospitalized	3	2	1
Trauma of abuse (physical, emotional, verbal and/or sexual)	3	2	1
Substance abuse	3	2	1
Being bullied	3	2	1
Health problems or chronic pain	3	2	1
Loss of friends, family members, pet	3	2	1
Peer Pressure	3	2	1
Illegal activities	3	2	1
Insecurity about the future	3	2	1
Arguments	3	2	1
Change in relationship with family and friends	3	2	1
Feeling bad for no known reason at all	3	2	1

PAGE 1 – TOTAL = _____

(Continued on the next page)

Mood Triggers Scale *(Continued)*

Additional factors that trigger my moodiness:	A Lot	Some	No Effect
Inability to forgive others	3	2	1
Fear	3	2	1
Loss of loved one	3	2	1
Shame and/or embarrassment	3	2	1
Rejected by friends	3	2	1
Feelings of being a victim	3	2	1
Feeling different than others	3	2	1
Feelings of hopelessness	3	2	1
Lack of privacy	3	2	1
Negative thoughts in my head	3	2	1
Need for independence	3	2	1
Not respected by adults in my life	3	2	1
Over critical of myself	3	2	1
Unresolved anger	3	2	1
View of myself	3	2	1
Fear of being a failure	3	2	1
Focus on the negative	3	2	1
Feelings of rebellion	3	2	1
Loneliness	3	2	1
Feelings of being judged	3	2	1
Feeling like life is not fair	3	2	1
Unhappy when I look in the mirror	3	2	1

PAGE 2 – TOTAL = _____

Go to the Scoring Directions on the next page

Mood Triggers Scale
Scoring Directions

Add the numbers you circled on both scales and write those scores on the lines marked TOTAL. Then, transfer those totals to the spaces below:

PAGE 1 = _____

PAGE 2 = _____
_____

TOTAL SCALE SCORE = _____

Profile Interpretation

Scale Score	Result	Indications
44 to 72	Low	Low scores indicate that you do not experience moodiness from these types of triggers.
73 to 103	Moderate	Moderate scores indicate that you experience some moodiness from these types of triggers.
104 to 132	High	High scores indicate that you experience a great deal of moodiness from these types of triggers.

No matter how you scored, low, moderate or high, you will benefit from these exercises. By completing the activities that follow, you will better understand the impact of internal and external triggers in your life.

Scale Description

People scoring high on this scale tend to experience moodiness as a result of occurrences in their environment (a loss, health issues, bullying, family, friends and school problems). They also tend to experience moodiness as a result of the feelings that are generated from their own negative thinking. They tend to think like victims and focus on the negative aspects of any situation.

Mood Triggers

My Mood Patterns

When do you get moody? It is helpful to think about how to recognize and deal with your patterns of moodiness.

Think about when you begin to feel moody and answer the questions that follow:

At what times do you begin to feel moody? _____
_____
_____

What is the association between the occurrence of stressful events and the onset of your moodiness? What are examples of these events? _____
_____
_____

Describe the situations in which your moodiness is intensified. _____
_____
_____

How does the weather affect your moodiness? Describe types of weather and how these weather types affect you? _____
_____
_____

Is your moodiness connected to drinking and/or substance abuse? Describe. _____
_____
_____

Is your moodiness connected to your eating habits and sleeping? Describe. _____
_____
_____

How and when does your moodiness occur? For no reason at all? As a result of an event or episode? Explain. _____
_____
_____

Early Warning Signs

The symptoms of moodiness might come and go throughout your life. This is okay if you know how to manage your symptoms effectively. To do this you need to recognize your symptoms. If you are able to notice early changes in your mood, you can take action. In the table below, explore how you usually feel and then how you feel when you are beginning to experience a mood change.

Symptom	How I Usually Feel When I'm Not Moody	How I Feel When I Am Becoming Moody
Example: General mood	I am pretty optimistic.	I see the negative side of everything.
General mood		
Hope about my future		
Social activity		
Physical Activity		
Sleeping habits		
Eating habits		
Religious Activity		
Self-esteem		
Spiritual Activity		
Ability to concentrate		
Illegal Activities		

(Continued on the next page)

Mood Triggers

Early Warning Signs *(Continued)*

Symptom	How I Usually Feel When I'm Not Moody	How I Feel When I Am Becoming Moody
Energy level		
Irritability level		
Decision-making ability		
Thoughts about harming yourself and others		
Problems in school		
Have fun and laugh		
Self-confidence		
Disagreements with family members		
Ability to tolerate frustration		
Stress Management		
Thoughts about suicide		

I'm Overwhelmed and Stressed

Teens get overwhelmed by juggling the time they devote to family, friends, school, homework, jobs and volunteering. Often, this is the result of trying to live up to their own high expectations, as well as the expectations of others. Being overwhelmed can definitely affect moodiness.

Below are some tips to avoid feeling overwhelmed:
- You do not need to be all things to all people.
- Recognize that you are feeling overwhelmed and prioritize. Now, later, tomorrow, whenever.
- Prioritize your interests and drop any extra activities that you no longer enjoy. If working on a task, break the task into smaller, more manageable steps.
- Take time to nurture and re-energize yourself and do safe, healthy things you love to do. Then, tackle what needs to be done.
- Monitor your internal thinking for thoughts such as "I should join the _____ club because it will look good on my community college application." Thoughts that include the words "should," "could," and "ought" can keep you feeling overwhelmed.
- Exercise to release tension.
- Set realistic goals for yourself when it comes to work, school, and family.
- Build a network of trusted friends and family members who can help you cope.
- Don't let being overwhelmed and stressed affect your eating or sleeping routines.
- Don't panic – take deep breaths and regroup.
- Practice relaxation techniques (meditation, deep breathing, guided imagery, etc.)

What Overwhelms Me	How It Overwhelms Me	What I Can Do About It
Example: Too much to get all A's.	I become anxious and I seem to do worse.	Prioritize and get the best grades I can get.

Reduce Moodiness with Exercise

The more teens play video and cell phone games, text, surf the Internet, etc., the less they are exercising. Exercising is one of the best ways to reduce the effects of moodiness.

When using exercise as a way to reduce your moodiness, keep several things in mind:
- First, check with your physician if you have a health issue.
- Begin now and continue on a regular schedule.
- Choose activities that will reduce moodiness but not be so strenuous that they cause stress.
- If you are playing in a competitive game, don't worry about the score or who wins or loses; play for the fun, relaxation and teamwork. Then enjoy it if you win!
- Start slowly and build up endurance over time.

In the spaces that follow, identify types of exercises you have already tried. State how you felt before engaging in them and how you felt afterwards.

Form of Exercising	How I Felt Before	How I Felt Afterwards
Walk		
Jog		
Ride a Bicycle		
Dance		
Yoga		
Swim		
Hike		
Ski/Toboggan/Skate		
Sports		
Chores Around the House		
Work Out		
Aerobics		
Martial Arts		
Other		

Put a check by the activities you will consider doing soon.

You Are What You Eat

In the case of moodiness, people are often really what they eat. Many teens don't eat very healthy foods, and a proper food regimen is critical in balancing emotional health. During moody periods, teens usually eat more unbalanced snacks or fast-food meals than usual. One way of managing triggers to moodiness is to maintain a well-balanced way of eating.

TIPS

- Reduce your fat intake, but be sure the fats you intake are healthy fats
- Avoid alcohol intake
- Reduce your use of caffeine
- Reduce the amount of sugar you eat and drink
- Eat more fruits and vegetables
- Eat a lot of grains (rye, oats, wheat, etc.)
- Eat protein-rich foods (beans and peas, lean beef, low-fat cheese, milk, poultry, soy products, yogurt)
- Eat plenty of fish (not fried)
- When you go to a fast-food chain, find one that features healthy foods.

What types of foods do you eat too much of when you are *in a bad mood*?
_____
_____

How does this kind of food make you feel?
_____
_____

What types of foods do you not eat enough of when you are *in a bad mood*?
_____
_____

How does this kind of food make you feel?
_____
_____

What changes can you make to practice a well-balanced way of eating, moody or not?
_____
_____
_____

Relaxation Techniques

Relaxation techniques can provide immediate benefits when one begins to feel mood changes. Consider a variety of techniques that may help you relax. Below are a few. There are many relaxation techniques on reliable Internet sources.

Deep Breathing – Deep breathing involves inhaling slowly through your nose (you should notice your abdomen going up and down) and exhaling through your mouth. Repeat this process by continuing to take long, slow deep breaths that raise and lower your abdomen. Continue this process for at least five to ten minutes or until your mood has lightened. Now you try it. Then describe below how you felt during the deep breathing exercise.

_____

_____

_____

_____

Light – Light can be extremely beneficial in reversing a bad mood. Try to spend at least a half an hour per day outside in the sunlight. You can simply walk or relax in a lounge chair. Remember that too much sunlight can be bad for your skin, so be careful. You may also want to ensure that the rooms in your house are well lit. Then describe below how you felt during your time in the sunshine and light.

_____

_____

_____

_____

Meditation – Meditation can help you to focus your attention on one thing at a time and keep outside influences away. For example, you could take a few minutes and gaze at an object of your choice (a candle, cup, flower, etc.) at your eye level. Gaze at the object for a few minutes. Note its size, shape and color. If you become distracted, simply return your gaze to the object. You could also count your breaths by counting one for each time you inhale and two when you exhale. Continue counting your breaths until you reach ten, and then begin again with one. Try it and describe below what happened to you – the thoughts running through your head – and your mood.

_____

_____

_____

_____

Research guided imagery/visualization as an excellent technique

That's Funny

Having a good sense of humor can help to maintain a positive perspective. Humor has been referred to as a natural antidote to moodiness.

Have fun when you are with other people. What can you do to have safe, healthy fun?

_____
_____
_____

See the funny side of a not-so-funny situation. What is a past situation could you flip around so that it becomes funny now?

_____
_____
_____

Laugh at situations involving yourself, either when something happens, or later, when you look back on it. If you do something silly, don't be afraid to laugh at yourself. What is an event that happened to you that was funny a while later as you told the story?

_____
_____
_____

It is good to laugh **with** others about **situations**. Why should you not laugh **at** other **people**?

_____
_____
_____

Take yourself and life more lightly. Try to stop seeing some situations so seriously. What types of situations do you take way too seriously?

_____
_____
_____

Watch humorous movies or television shows. What are your favorites? Compare with others in the room. Make a group list.

_____
_____
_____

Mood Triggers

My Reactions When I'm Moody

When suffering with moodiness, we often react in ways we wouldn't ordinarily.

In the sentence starters below, write about ways you react. USE NAME CODES.

When I feel overwhelmed, I _____
_____
_____

When I am all alone, I _____
_____
_____

When I am being ignored, I _____
_____
_____

When I am feeling frustrated, I _____
_____
_____

When I am physically ill, I _____
_____
_____

When I'm with _____ I _____
_____
_____

With whom can you talk with when you feel moody? _____

My Internal Triggers

Some internal triggers of moodiness are the result of one's own thinking. Thoughts can influence how one feels! It is helpful to be aware of how thinking can trigger moodiness.

Following are some of the different types of negative thinking patterns that might be affecting how you feel. USE NAME CODES.

Labeling – In this type of thinking, one attaches a negative label to oneself or to others. Examples include "I'm a terrible friend" or "He's stupid." What are some of the labels you call yourself?

_____

_____

In your mind, what do you call others? _____

_____

Tyranny of "Would" "Should" and "Could" – In this type of thinking, one keeps thinking about how things could, should or would have been done. What are some of the "would of" "should of" and/or "could of" words you use for yourself and for other people?

_____

_____

_____

Tuning In – In this type of thinking, one focuses on the negative aspects of a situation or aspects about oneself and ignores the positive aspects. Provide an example of a time you have done this.

_____

_____

_____

Make a Mountain out of a Molehill – In this type of thinking, one makes events and situations out of proportion, often because of a lack of adequate information. An example of this is when one doesn't make the soccer team and thinks her world is over. What types of situations or events trigger this sort of thinking in you?

_____

_____

**Make an effort to eliminate these negative patterns from your thinking.
It will make a difference!**

Mood Triggers

Victim Thinking

Because many of the internal triggers of moodiness are the result of victim thinking, one can control these triggers by learning more effective ways of thinking.

Here are some of the more effective ways of controlling internal triggers due to victim thinking.

Type	When I Do This	How I Can Change This Type of Thinking
Overthinking – *Example: I am often unsure of myself and I keep thinking and dwelling about any issue of any kind.*		
Worrying – *Example: I have such low self-confidence, I continually worry about things, even if they are out of my control and/or unrealistic.*		
Pessimistic thinking – *Example: I honestly believe that nothing good will ever happen to me.*		
Feelings of being blamed – *Example: I feel like people blame me first when anything goes wrong.*		
Other: _____ _____ _____		

Which of the types above best describes you? Who is a trusted person you can talk with about this, to develop a plan of controlling this internal trigger?

_____

_____

Worry, Worry, Worry

Anyone can become moody just by worrying about events that may or may not occur in the future. The problem with worrying is that very often the event is not as bad as one imagines it to be and probably all the worry was for nothing. Even if there is a problem, worrying and/or being out of control does not help the situation.

Identify those times in your life when you worried more than needed. USE NAME CODES.

Events	My Worrying Thoughts	How I Handled It	The Outcome of the Situation	Another Way to Have Handled It
Example: Going to the prom.	People will laugh at the way I dance.	I tried to think of a way of getting out of my commitment, so I went.	I didn't dance and had very little fun.	I might have asked my sister to teach me a few basic dance steps.

"If a problem is fixable, if a situation is such that you can do something about it, then there is no need to worry. If it's not fixable, then there is no help in worrying. There is no benefit in worrying whatsoever."

~Dalai Lama XIV

Mood Triggers

Feeling Good About Myself

Moodiness can have a negative effect on how and what people think about themselves and their self-esteem. It can trigger feelings so that they believe that they are different from others, or that they feel they can't reach their goals. It can magnify fears of interacting with others or becoming intimate with people.

What and how you think about yourself can have an extremely positive or an extremely negative effect on your moods.

Some Ways to Boost Your Self-Esteem

Take part in community activities.

- Activities I already take part in: _____
  _____
  _____

- Activities I would like to take part in: _____
  _____
  _____

Choose work or a volunteer job that you will enjoy.

- Work or volunteer job I might like to do or might enjoy: _____
  _____
  _____

- Work or volunteer job I already enjoy: _____
  _____
  _____

Participate in activities in which you feel good about yourself.

- Activities in which I enjoy: _____
  _____
  _____

- Activities in which I do not enjoy: _____
  _____
  _____

(Continued on the next page)

Feeling Good About Myself *(Continued)*

Identify your achievements.

- Some of my best achievements: _____
_____
_____

Think about the kind of work you have done.

- My accomplishments: _____
_____
_____

- Goals I have for my career: _____
_____
_____

Think about your educational achievements.

- My educational accomplishments: _____
_____
_____

- Goals I have for further education or learning: _____
_____
_____

Express yourself creatively.

- My creative accomplishments: _____
_____
_____

- Goals I have for additional creations: _____
_____
_____

MODULE IV
Roller Coaster Moods

*I know without treatment
I would have never been able to
harness my creativity in such a
successful way.*

~ Patty Duke

Name _____

Date _____

Managing Moods

Roller Coaster Moods Scale
Introduction and Directions

Teens often feel a wide range of mood swings. This can be due to biological, hormonal, chemical imbalance reasons – or – just being a teenager. If your moods are happy, and then soon after, sad and depressed, you may be experiencing life like a rollercoaster.

The *Roller Coaster Moods Scale* can help you explore, if at times your moods are like a carousel – whose horses go up and down slightly, or if they are more like a steep, sharply curved roller coaster – very high and then very low. Either way, learning to manage your moods will be helpful.

This scale contains 20 statements. Read each of the statements and decide how descriptive the statement is of you. In each of the choices listed, circle the number of your response to the right of each statement.

In the following example, the circled 1 indicates that the statement is not at all descriptive of the person completing the inventory:

4 = Very Descriptive   **3 = Somewhat Descriptive**   **2 = A Little Descriptive**   **1 = Not At All Descriptive**

At times ...

I get just a few hours of sleep 4   3   2   (1)

This is not a test and there are no right or wrong answers. Do not spend too much time thinking about your answers. Your initial response will be the most true for you. Be sure to respond to every statement.

Turn to the next page and begin.

Managing Moods

Roller Coaster Moods Scale

| 4 = Very Descriptive | 3 = Somewhat Descriptive | 2 = A Little Descriptive | 1 = Not At All Descriptive |

At times…

I get just a few hours of sleep	4	3	2	1
There are times I just can't calm down	4	3	2	1
I am impulsive and rowdy	4	3	2	1
I am loud and laugh at inappropriate times	4	3	2	1
I am much more interested in sex than usual	4	3	2	1
I feel more self-confident than usual	4	3	2	1
I feel invincible	4	3	2	1
I feel too good	4	3	2	1
I want to keep moving	4	3	2	1
I have sudden, unusual bursts of enthusiasm	4	3	2	1
I seek thrills I don't normally seek	4	3	2	1
I feel "out of control"	4	3	2	1
I am more talkative than usual	4	3	2	1
I use poor judgment	4	3	2	1
I spend money foolishly	4	3	2	1
I feel unrealistically optimistic	4	3	2	1
I feel like others are moving in slow motion	4	3	2	1
I notice my ideas race around in my head	4	3	2	1
I have surges of energy	4	3	2	1
I feel very restless	4	3	2	1

TOTAL = _____

Go to the Scoring Directions on the next page

Roller Coaster Moods Scale
Scoring Directions

It is important to measure the level of your mood stabilities and instabilities and to be able to maintain and manage them.

Count the scores you circled and place that number on the line marked TOTAL at the end of the assessment. Then, transfer your total to the space below:

ROLLER COASTER MOODS TOTAL   =   _____

Profile Interpretation

Scale Score	Result	Indications
20 to 30	Low	Low scores indicate that you exhibit subtle bouts of mood instability with slight carousel ups and downs.
31 to 60	Moderate	Moderate scores indicate that you exhibit some roller coaster moods.
61 to 80	High	High scores indicate that you exhibit intense bouts of mood instability with roller coaster highs and lows.

Scale Description

People with high scores will typically have periods of time when they feel down and depressed even though it seems as if there's no reason at all. Other times they may be extremely upbeat, with unusually high energy.

Managing Moods

Over-Excited? Frantic? Frenzied? Agitated?

It is helpful to think about the patterns of roller coaster moods. Think about when you begin to feel over-excited, frantic, frenzied and or agitated and answer the questions that follow. Use Name Codes.

What types of changes in your life affect you in the same way as the moods in the title of this page?

_____

_____

_____

What is the association between the occurrence of a stressful event and the onset of these moods? What are these events?

_____

_____

_____

If you take medications, what is the association of your taking the meds, or not taking the meds, and the onset of these moods?

_____

_____

_____

What are the situations (at, school, home, work/volunteer, community, etc.) in which these moods are intensified? Describe what you are doing when your mood is the most intense?

_____

_____

_____

In what ways do changes in relationships affect or bring on these moods?

_____

_____

_____

What have trusted others told you about your reactions or moods?

_____

_____

_____

Recognizing Symptoms

To effectively manage symptoms of being on the very low or very high side of a roller coaster, it is important to recognize those symptoms emerging. By recognizing early changes in your mood, one can take action to cope more effectively.

In the table below, explore how you normally feel and then how you feel when you begin to experience roller coaster highs. USE NAME CODES.

Symptom	Situation	Example of My Reaction
Example: I am more impatient than usual.	When I am ready to go out and my dinner isn't ready.	I scream at GRW and won't talk to him for a few days.
I am more impatient than usual		
I stay awake all night working on something		
Everything seems like a hassle		
I am happier than usual		
I have an unusually positive outlook		
I am more talkative and talk faster than usual		
I have an inappropriate sense of humor		
I lose my focus easily		
I take unhealthy risks		
I can't concentrate on what I need to do		

(Continued on the next page)

Managing Moods

Recognizing Symptoms *(Continued)*

Symptom	Moderate Symptoms	Severe Symptoms
I am overly self-confident		
Any change sounds possible		
I have too many creative thoughts whirling around		
I am too fidgety to sit still		
I am extremely anxious		
I bite my nails and/or pick my cuticles		
I am more creative than usual		
I have amazing, but not always possible ideas		
I am uncomfortable with others		
I lose my train of thought easily		
I find everyone annoying		
Other _____		

It will we helpful, if you are comfortable, to ask a TRUSTED ADULT to review these two pages and tell you whether he/she agrees with how you react.

Major Life Decisions

When faced with early warning signs of mood instability, it is beneficial to avoid making important life decisions. Decisions that could affect one's life and others around that person need to be postponed until one feels balanced and in control.

In the table below, identify major life decisions that are approaching, and how you will make each of your decisions. USE NAME CODES.

Major Life Decisions	How I Will Go About Making a Decision	How I Will Know I Am in Control
Something Risky – *Example: I am thinking about quitting school.*	*I will talk with MGF about the decision.*	*When I am feeling even-keeled, I will review the pros and cons of this.*
People at Home		
School		
Friends		
Somethig Risky		
Major Purchase		
Other		

Managing Moods

To Take or Not To Take?

In managing mood instability, it is important to take medications regularly, and as directed. One of the biggest problems of people who have roller coaster ups-and-downs is that as soon as they feel somewhere between the very highs and the very lows, they think they're okay, and stop taking their meds. They forget that without their meds, highs will go to lows and then to highs again. If they had cancer, diabetes, or an infection, they would take their meds as long as they needed. Roller-coaster moods are no different – the meds are important as prescribed. They can be extremely helpful, but they may also have unwanted side affects, which can deter people from taking them. It is important to talk to physicians, research ways to deal with side affects and learn which reactions to report immediately.

In the table below, identify all of the medications you have taken and are currently taking; how regularly you take them; the side effects; how you can minimize those side effects; and how the meds help you. Include both medications prescribed by a physician as well as over-the-counter medicines.

My Medications	Take Regularly?	Side Effects	How I Can Minimize the Side-Effects	How the Meds Help Me

If you have stopped taking them, why?
_____
_____

Have you spoken to your physician about this? If not, why not?
_____
_____

What medication changes or additions do you need to speak about with your physician?
_____
_____

Take this completed paper with you to your medical professional on your next visit.

Roller Coaster Moods

Outlets for Excessive Energy

It is often a challenge to find healthy outlets (and we don't mean the outlet mall) for your excessive energy, but it is well worth it.

In the table below, explore healthy ways to channel your energy into hobbies, physical and recreational activities, and social activities. USE NAME CODES.

My Healthy Outlets	My Unhealthy Outlets
In School I …	In School I …
Physically I …	Physically I …
Socially I …	Socially I …
Mentally I …	Mentally I …

What can you do to actively participate in more healthy outlets?

School _____

Physically _____

Socially _____

Mentally _____

Managing Moods

Damage-Repair

Roller coaster ups-and-downs will often affect relationships with friends and family members! It is important to try to stay focused on relationships. Keeping moodiness management goals in mind and remember that one can work to repair damaged relationships. Life will get better!

In the table that follows, write about the relationships you have damaged in the midst of mood instabilities. USE NAME CODES.

The Person and Our Relationship	How I Have Damaged the Relationship	How I Can Possibly Repair the Damage
Example: JKL	I have encouraged him to drink alcohol so that I would have someone to drink with and to be cool with.	Apologize to JKL and talk to him about the impact of my roller-coaster mood swings. I hope he will understand and forgive me.

Most people will forgive others once or twice. Keeping promises, staying under control and taking meds regularly will ensure the lasting quality of a relationship.

Roller Coaster Moods

My WEEKLY Mood Chart

People who experience mood instabilities are often unaware of how quickly and how often their moods go up or down from week to week. A Weekly Mood Chart is simply a diary of your mood patterns.

This activity will help you to identify when your mood instabilities occur and when you need to implement your coping mechanisms. USE NAME CODES.

Time Frame: _____

Day of the Week	Daily Notes of Mood-Related Issues or Instabilities	Hours Slept	General Mood (Up, down, sad, happy, etc.)	4 if meds were taken
Monday				
Tuesday				
Wednesday				
Thursday				
Friday				
Saturday				
Sunday				

Notes _____

Managing Moods

My DAILY Mood Chart

People who experience mood instabilities are often unaware of how quickly and how often their moods are unstable, going up and down, from hour to hour. A Daily Mood Chart is simply a diary of your mood patterns.

This activity will help you to identify when your mood instabilities occur and when you need to implement your coping mechanisms. USE NAME CODES.

Date _____   Day of the Week _____

Time of the Day	Daily Note of Mood-Related Issues or Instabilities	Hours Slept	General Mood (Up, down, sad, happy, etc.)	4 if meds were taken
7:00 am – 9:00 am				
9:00 am – Noon				
Noon – 3:00 pm				
3:00 pm – 6:00 pm				
6:00 pm – 9:00 pm				
9:00 pm – Midnight				
Midnight – 2:00 am				
2:00 am – 7:00 am				

Notes

Roller Coaster Moods

Potential Support Network

Educating (talking about one's moods) and involving (asking for support) one's significant others, family members and trusted friends and adults about roller coaster moods can be unbelievably helpful. In addition, one can involve these important people in treatment when possible. They can help spot symptoms, track behaviors, gain perspective, remind one to take meds, accompany one to appointments, provide encouraging feedback, and help make a plan to cope with any future crises.

Who are the significant others, family members and trusted friends and adults with whom you feel safe in confiding and who can support you? In the table below, identify those people and how they can support you. Some people can support in one way (listening) and others can support in other ways (encouraging). Think about each person and how you can benefit from that person's particular strengths. USE NAME CODES.

Potential Supportive Person	How and What Will I Tell This Person About Me and My Needs	How This Person Can Support Me

Which one of the people above will you contact first? _____

When? _____

Managing Moods

My Impulsive Up-Side Behaviors

It is important to identify impulsive behaviors when experiencing the upside of your roller-coaster moods. Impulsive behaviors are usually risky behaviors and might include alcohol, drugs, thrills, gambling, abusing meds, spending money, sex, etc.

In the table below, explore your behavior. USE NAME CODES.

My Behavior	My Usual Behavior	My Impulsive Behavior
Example: I drive when I am with JRE.	I drive carefully – I don't want to look responsible	I drive very fast to show off, even if roads are slippery.

TIPS For Overcoming Impulsive Behavior:

Avoid situations that will put you at risk. What are those situations for you? _____
_____
_____

Spend time with people you know and trust. Who are those people? _____
_____
_____

Try to relax. What are some healthy ways that you could relax? _____
_____

Roller Coaster Moods

My Social Rhythms – WeekDAYS

Teens with roller coaster moods are believed to have very sensitive social rhythms, or life patterns. This social rhythm can easily be thrown off by disruptions in daily patterns of activity. When these social rhythms are stable, the biological rhythms that regulate mood remain stable too.

List the times you engage in these activities during the day. Reproduce this sheet for each day of the week.
TODAY: _____

Activity	My Usual Time	My "Down Days" Time	My "Up Days" Time
Example: Get out of bed	6:30 a.m.	11 a.m.	1 or 2 a.m.
Get out of bed			
Morning rituals			
Interact with anyone			
Eat breakfast			
Take a.m. meds & supplements			
Get ready for the day			
Go to school/work			
Interact with people			
Have lunch			
After school activities			
Ride home from school			
Eat dinner			
Do homework			
Text, email, etc.			
Evening activities			
Eat late night snack			
Pre-bedtime rituals			
Take bedtime meds			
Bedtime			

What did you learn about the stability of your everyday routines? _____

Continued on the next page

Managing Moods

My Social Rhythms – WeekENDS

Teens with roller coaster moods are believed to have very sensitive social rhythms, or life patterns. This social rhythm can easily be thrown off by disruptions by weekend patterns of activity. When these social rhythms are stable, the biological rhythms that regulate mood remain stable too.

List the times you engage in these activities on the weekends. Reproduce this sheet for additional weekend days. Weekend day_____

Activity	My Usual Time	My "Down Days" Time	My "Up Days" Time
Example: Get out of bed	*8:30 a.m.*	*2 p.m.*	*9:30 a.m.*
Get out of bed			
Morning rituals			
Interact with anyone			
Eat breakfast			
Take a.m. meds & supplements			
Get ready for the day			
Go to work / other			
Interact with people			
Have lunch			
Afternoon activities			
Eat dinner			
Do homework			
Text, email, etc.			
Evening activities			
Eat late night snack			
Pre-bedtime rituals			
Take bedtime meds			
Bedtime			

What did you learn about the stability of your everyday routines on the weekends?_____
_____
_____

Roller Coaster Moods

Activity vs. Inactivity

In working to manage and/or overcome mood instabilities and their effects, it is important to find the right balance between activity and inactivity. This can be difficult because our body may be telling us that we are too tired to do ANYTHING or it may be telling to do EVERYTHING!

You need to seek balance. Overstimulation by more activities than you can handle easily might trigger an uncomfortable situation. USE NAME CODES.

Aspect of My Life	Activities in Which I'm Involved	Activities I Could Change
Example: school life	I am in 3 clubs and play on the tennis team.	I could eliminate one of them and balance my time better.
School life		
Community life		
Work life		
Family relationships		
Volunteering		
Time with friends		
Clubs & organizations		
Entertainment		
Dating relationships		
Other		

Which of these changes seems doable? Which of these changes sounds difficult?

Managing Moods

Predictable and Unpredictable Changes

Changes in a routine can bring on moodiness and mood instabilities. Changes in a routine can be either predictable or unpredictable. Predictable changes include graduating high school, going to college and/or finding a job. These types of changes are usually easier to adjust to.

Think about the upcoming changes you know about and how you will prepare to maintain your social rhythms and stability. USE NAME CODES.

Predictable Changes Coming Up in My Routine	How They Will Disrupt My Rhythm	What I Will Do To Adapt

Unpredictable changes include being fired from a job, a sudden death or an unexpected illness. These types of changes are harder to adjust to.

Think back on the unpredicted changes you have experienced and how they affected you and your ability to maintain your social rhythms and stability, and what you learned about yourself.
USE NAME CODES.

Unpredictable Changes in My Routine from the Past	How They Affected Me and My Stability and Social Rhythms	What I Learned About Myself to Remember for the Future

Listening

> **Lord Beaverbrook said about Winston Churchill:**
> *"What a creature of strange moods."*

What strange moods do you have?

_____
_____
_____
_____
_____
_____
_____
_____
_____
_____

What is your action plan to ensure that you are comfortable with your moods?

_____
_____
_____
_____
_____
_____
_____
_____
_____
_____
_____

MODULE V

Erasing the Stigma of Mental Health Issues

Mental illness is nothing to be ashamed of, but stigma and bias shames us all.

~ President William J. Clinton

Name _____

Date _____

Erasing the Stigma of Mental Health Issues
Introduction

A stigma is extreme social disapproval of some type of personal characteristic or a belief that is not considered socially "acceptable." People who have a particular attribute considered unwanted by society are rejected or stigmatized as a result of the attribute. People who experience bouts of moodiness are often judged unfairly to be violent, unpredictable, explosive, aggressive and/or unstable. These judgments, or social stigmas, can cause people who experience moodiness to feel devalued as human beings. They are often ostracized from activities, rejected in social situations, stereotyped, minimized in the workplace, and shunned by others. People experiencing the stigma of moodiness often feel extreme physical and psychological distress.

People who stigmatize and/or stereotype others bring about unfair treatment rather than help. This unfair treatment can be very obvious. For example, people make negative comments or laugh. On the other hand, this unfair treatment can be very subtle. For example, people assume that a moody person is dangerous or violent, and they avoid or shun that person.

Stigmas affect a large percentage of people throughout the world. Some of the more common stigmas are associated with physical disabilities, mental health issues, age, body type, gender, sexual orientation, nationality, religion, family, ethnicity, race, religion, financial status, social sub-cultures and conduct. Stigmas set people apart from society and produce feelings in them of shame and isolation. People who are stigmatized are often considered socially unacceptable and they suffer prejudice, rejection, avoidance and discrimination.

What Can Be Done?

Fear of judgment and ridicule about moodiness often compels individuals and their families to hide away from society rather than face criticism, shunning, labeling and stereotyping. Instead of seeking treatment, they struggle in silence. Let's discuss some ways you can combat the stereotypes and stigmas that are associated with moodiness.

- You and your loved ones have choices. You can decide who is to know about your moodiness and what to tell them. You need not feel ashamed or embarrassed.

- You are not alone. Remember that many other people are coping with a similar situation.

- Seek help and remember that the activities in this workbook and treatment from medical professionals can help you to have a productive education and career, and live satisfying lives.

- Be proactive and surround yourself with supportive people – people you can trust. Social isolation is a negative side effect of the stigma linked to moodiness. Isolating yourself and discontinuing enjoyable activities will not help.

How Can This Section Help Me?

The *Managing Moods Workbook for Teens* is designed to help you deal more effectively with your moodiness, and this section is specifically designed to help you overcome the stigma attached to moodiness. Complete the activities that follow to feel better about yourself, feel content, and become more resilient in the face of stress in your life.

Two Types of Mental Health Stigma

Mental health stigma can be divided into two types:

1. **Social stigma** is characterized by prejudicial attitudes and discriminating behavior directed towards individuals with mental health problems.
2. **Perceived stigma** is the internalizing by the people with mental health conditions of their understanding of discrimination.

Name some incidents when you felt people were judging you, talking about you or discriminating against you because of your moodiness. Next to your description of the incident, mark a number 1 or number 2, to indicate whether it was a social stigma or a perceived stigma. If you're not sure which, mark it with a question mark. USE NAME CODES.

_____
_____
_____
_____
_____
_____
_____
_____
_____
_____
_____
_____
_____
_____
_____
_____
_____

Often one perceives others' stigmatizing, or exaggerates others' or their own reactions.

Erasing the Stigma of Mental Health Issues

The Stigma of Being Known as "Moody" – THE PAST

Moodiness can strike anyone! Mental health issues know no limits. During the course of a year, one or more mental health issue such as moodiness, will affect millions and millions of people.

Often the stigma attached to moodiness stops one from moving forward – being unable to talk about it for fear of being judged or labeled. We can erase the stigma of any mental health issues by starting to discuss it with one person at a time, and taking the time to explain thoughts and feelings.

Let's start with whom you have already shared. USE NAME CODES.

With Whom Have You Discussed Your Moody Behaviors?	What Did You Say?	What Was This Person's Reaction? What Did the Person Say?	How Did You Feel?
Family			
Friends			
Acquaintances			
Teachers, Coaches and/or Other School Administrators			
School Counselor and/or Mental Health Professional			
Other			

If any one of the above reacted in a negative way, to what do you attribute that reaction?

_____

_____

_____

The Stigma of Being Known as "Moody" – THE PRESENT

People often have perceptions about people who are moody. One of the ways to erase this stigma is to talk about it and let others know that people who are moody are just like anyone else who have some type of a condition.

Perhaps it is time to talk with other people whom you trust and/or with whom you feel safe.
USE NAME CODES.

Person with whom you might discuss your moody behaviors	What would you say to this person?	What do you think this person's reaction might be?	What could you gain or lose by discussing it with this person?
Family			
Friends			
Acquaintances			
Teachers, Coaches and/or Other School Administrators			
School Counselor and/or Mental Health Professional			
Others			

Brainstorm with the group:
At what point, in a serious relationship, is it time to discuss your moodiness issues?

Erasing the Stigma of Mental Health Issues

What Animal are YOU?

> *Animals don't lie. Animals don't criticize. If animals have moody days, they handle them better than humans do.*
>
> *~ Betty White*

When you are in a moody frame of mind, what animal do you resemble?

_____

How do you resemble that animal? _____

_____

_____

How do people react to this animal-like behavior? _____

_____

_____

When you are NOT in a moody frame of mind, what animal do you resemble?

_____

How do you resemble that animal? _____

_____

_____

How do people react to this animal-like behavior? _____

_____

_____

Which animal do you like better and why? _____

_____

_____

If We Stamp Out the Stigma ...

Journal your thoughts about the following quotation:

If we stamp out the stigma attached to mental health issues, shed the shame and eliminate the fear, then we open the door for people to speak freely about what they are feeling and thinking.

~ Jaletta Albright Desmond

Erasing the Stigma of Mental Health Issues

Glenn Close said ...

"The most powerful way to change someone's view is to meet them ... People who do come out and talk about mental illness, that's when healing can really begin. You can lead a productive life."

Use Name Codes.

Name a time when you have changed someone else's view – about anything. _____
_____
_____

How did that feel to you? _____
_____
_____

Name a time you were tempted to talk about your moodiness issue, but didn't? Why not? _____
_____
_____

Write about a situation in which you DID talk about your moodiness condition. _____
_____
_____

How did that feel? _____

How did it work out? _____
_____

Who is a trusted person you can talk with, to begin to heal? _____

Anyone else? _____

Who is a trusted person you can ask for a referral of someone to talk with, to begin to heal? _____
_____

Anyone else? _____

In an ideal world, how can you lead a more stable life? _____
_____
_____

How can you contribute to changing stigma? _____
_____
_____

Effects of the Stigma of Moodiness

Check out these harmful effects of the stigma of being moody and write on the lines next to each item if it has affected you in some way and how. USE NAME CODES.

1. Lack of understanding by family _____

2. Lack of understanding by friends _____

3. Lack of understanding by teachers, coaches and/other school administrators _____

4. Discrimination at work or school _____

5. Inability to join clubs or organizations _____

6. Bullying; physical, emotional, verbal or sexual harassment_____

7. Peer pressure from friends _____

8. The belief that you will never be able to succeed or that you can't improve your situation. _____

On the line of the corresponding number, write the name of a person you can speak to, a person who might help to support you about each of the situations you noted above. Add a reason you've chosen that person.

1. _____
2. _____
3. _____
4. _____
5. _____
6. _____
7. _____
8. _____

Erasing the Stigma of Mental Health Issues

The Stigma of Going to a Mental Health Therapist

Many people have pre-conceived ideas about anyone seeking therapy.

Do you know of anyone who has gone to a mental health therapist? USE NAME CODES and write what you know about the experience. _____

_____

_____

Here are some facts about mental health and mental health therapy.

- Mental health includes how you act, feel and think in different situations.
- Mental health problems can be caused by many different things including medical health issues, abuse (emotional, physical, verbal, sexual), stress, worry, loss of a relationship, food issues, self-injuries, ADHD, STD's, family changes, addictions, traumatic event, problems, wanting to build up self-confidence, etc.
- If someone goes to a mental health therapist, this does NOT mean the person is crazy. Twenty percent of teens have mental health issues. Doctors and mental health therapists treat people the same as any other doctor treats problems (broken leg, diabetes, cancer, etc.).
- There needs to be a good connection between you and the therapist. Your therapist should be someone you feel you can trust.
- This might take a few meetings and/or a few therapists, to find the right one for you.
- Non-judgmental people who truly care about you will not judge you in a negative way. They will be proud of you for seeking help.
- The therapist does not assume that you have a mental illness. The therapist assumes something is troubling you, knows that no one leads a perfect life, and admires you for trying to make changes in your life.
- The therapist's job is to help you understand what's going on.
- The therapist will not tell you how to live your life, or how to think, act or believe.
- The therapist is not an advice-giver, but will help you think about how to increase your quality of life.
- The therapist may have some thoughts, and with you, will help you make changes.
- The therapist can help you to increase your life management skills.
- The therapist will help you recognize and express your feelings in a healthy way.
- The only person who can "fix" your problems is you, but a therapist will help you with an action plan.
- The mental health therapist may suggest that you see a medical doctor for medication.
- Therapy can be a slow or long process. Being open and honest, and wanting to feel better, will make the difference.

Place an X by the facts that you were not aware of.

What worries you about talking with a mental health therapist? _____

_____

After learning about these facts, can you make a commitment to speak with a counselor or therapist?

signature _____

Stereotypes

The social stigmas about moodiness often translate to the following inaccurate stereotypes.

In the table below, write about how you are unlike the stereotype provided.

Stereotype	How I Defy That Stereotype
People who are moody lack willpower.	
Moody people's emotions are always out of control.	
People who are moody are dangerous to themselves or others.	
Moody people are just whiney and make excuses.	
People who are moody are not very friendly.	
Other stereotypes of moody people.	

What would you like to say to other people who label you with these or other stereotypes?

_____

_____

_____

Erasing the Stigma of Mental Health Issues

Coping with the Stigma of Moodiness

The stigma of having a condition such as moodiness is often more damaging than the moodiness itself. Although we have come a long way, the acceptance of mental health issues is still a long way off.

Learning to cope with your moodiness and the stigma that surrounds it will be helpful. Use Name Codes.

People treat you a bit differently. They might think of you as fragile, not knowing what your mood might be like, and they might avoid you altogether. What can you do about that? Consider educating them about your moodiness. What could you say?

_____

_____

_____

Use your own discretion. It is important for you and your well-being to be educated about your mood issue and to decide on whether to share and/or educate others. Trust your instinct. Educate and share with others with whom you feel most comfortable and trust.

With whom are you comfortable telling about it and why?

_____

_____

With whom are you *not* comfortable telling about it and why?

_____

_____

Own your moodiness. Learn how to cope with it, dispel it and learn about it. What do you already know about it?

_____

_____

_____

Accept that you are special, worthwhile and have much to offer the world. Many famous people had the same condition (*example: Winston Churchill and Beethoven*). What famous contemporary people have you read or heard about, who have mood issues?

_____

_____

_____

Despite your moodiness, what is special about you and what do you have to offer to the world?

_____

_____

_____

What Can YOU Do?

"We have to get the word out that mental illnesses can be diagnosed and treated, and almost everyone suffering from mental illness can live meaningful lives in their communities."

~ *Rosalynn Carter*

How can YOU get the word out to erase the stigma of mental illness?

_____
_____
_____
_____
_____
_____
_____
_____
_____
_____

Brainstorm with a few other people how your group can get the word out to erase the stigma of mental illness?

_____
_____
_____
_____
_____
_____
_____
_____
_____
_____

Erasing the Stigma of Mental Health Issues

My Negative Thoughts

You can begin to overcome the stigma of moodiness by refusing to worry about what others think. When you are worried about what others say about you, or might say about you, you will have constant thoughts that stop you from enjoying life.

What are the negative thoughts that go through your head about others and what they think of you?

Others think I am …

_____
_____
_____

Others don't think I can …

_____
_____
_____

Others probably find me …

_____
_____
_____

I think others might be afraid or wary of me because …

_____
_____
_____

Others label me as …

_____
_____
_____

This makes me feel …

_____
_____
_____

Now that you have written these thoughts, take a big heavy black marker and put a big **X** through all of the thoughts above. When these negative thoughts come into your head, picture that big X, reminding you not to worry about what others think.

Focus on Your Strengths

You can do many things to help fight the stigma associated with moodiness. You can focus on your strengths rather than your limitations. Demonstrate to others, and yourself, that you have a great deal to offer.

In the spaces that follow, identify some of your strengths. You have much to share, so take a few minutes to think about and write about some of your greatest strengths.

My strengths related to school:

_____
_____
_____

My strengths related to relationships with others:

_____
_____
_____

My strengths related to my work or volunteer job:

_____
_____
_____

My strengths related to creativity:

_____
_____
_____

My strengths related to special skills I possess:

_____
_____
_____

How can you share these strengths to show others that even though you may be moody, you are still a capable, talented human being?

_____
_____
_____

Ways I Try to Minimize My Moodiness

Many teens dealing with moodiness will try a variety of ways to minimize the moodiness because of its stigma.

Complete the following table to explore the various ways that you minimize your moodiness, how this makes you feel, and describe some better ways to cope.

Ways I Minimize My Moodiness	The Affect This Has on Me and Others	A Better Way to Cope
Example: I pretend that nothing is wrong with me. I yell at BJ and then pretend that I am behaving just fine.	*BJ thinks I'm rude and doesn't want to be around me. I feel sad and ashamed.*	*Explain that I get moody at times and I'm working on it.*
I pretend that nothing is wrong with me		
I refuse to get help		
I say things like "Nothing can ever help me"		
I will not to talk about my issues		
I laugh and make jokes about my behavior		
I avoid people		
Other		
Other		

Ways I Am Treated

Think about some of the ways that people treat you because of your moodiness. In the spaces below, explore the various ways people treat you. Write about those who treat you unfairly and why.
USE NAME CODES.

I am rejected by family:
(*Example: MSE calls me names.*)

[   ]

I am rejected by my friends . . .

[   ]

I encounter problems at school . . .

[   ]

I encounter problems at home . . .

[   ]

I am subjected to physical violence or harassment . . .

[   ]

I am laughed at . . .

[   ]

I treat myself unfairly by . . .

[   ]

I treat myself fairly by . . .

[   ]

Erasing the Stigma of Mental Health Issues

Stay Active

Hiding away from other people because of moodiness does not help, nor will it show other people that moody people need support and understanding. It is important to remain active and continue participating in enjoyable activities.

In the table below, identify some of the activities you enjoy, but have stopped engaging in and why. USE NAME CODES.

Activity	Why I Stopped Doing It	How This Affected Me	What I Can Do in the Future
Example: Joining the basketball team	I threw a fit if we didn't win and everyone said that I took the game too seriously. They said I was a bad sport.	I quit the team and now I am sorry.	I will try to curb my frustration and will be a good sport.

Self-Doubt

Don't let stigma create self-doubt and shame. One of the most important ways to minimize the stigma of moodiness is to explore how one doubts oneself. Self-doubt almost always stems from a lack of understanding rather than information based on the facts. Feeling ashamed, embarrassed or humiliated because of a mood issue beyond your control can be very destructive.

How does your moodiness cause you to doubt yourself and how can you control your self-doubt in a positive and strong way? USE NAME CODES.

Ways I Doubt Myself	How This Negatively Affects Me	What I Can Do About it
Example: In class, I am afraid to answer questions because I might be wrong and people will laugh.	I sit in class, keep my eyes down so the teacher will not call on me, and say nothing.	I will not worry about what others say. The worst that can happen is that I give a wrong answer. So do others!

However you arrive at the ability to ignore self-doubt – if you can acquire it or possess it or find it or discover it – move beyond self-doubt.

~ Dwight Yoakum

How do you relate to this quotation? _____

_____

A Poster About the Stigma of Moodiness

In the space that follows, draw a collage of pictures, symbols and/or words of how you believe moodiness looks in people when they are stigmatized by others.

A Poster About Acceptance of People With Moodiness

In the space that follows, draw a collage of pictures, symbols and/or words of how you believe moodiness looks when people are accepted.

DE-STIGMA-TIZE with the Facts about Mental Health Issues

Myth: Mental health issues are rare.

Fact: Mental health issues are not rare and affect nearly everyone either directly or indirectly.

Myth: People with mental health issues are unable to lead productive lives.

Fact: Most people with a mental health issue respond to treatment, learn to cope with and manage their problems, and go on to lead productive and fulfilling lives.

Myth: People who have mental health conditions will not get better.

Fact: Once diagnosed, mental health issues are treatable. While they are not always cured, they can be managed effectively. Most people with mental health conditions live productive and positive lives while receiving treatments for their mental health issues. As is the case with any illness, individuals with severe or persistent mental health conditions who respond poorly to available treatments may require more support and may not function as highly as others.

Myth: People with serious mental health issues are violent and unpredictable.

Fact: While some people who suffer from serious mental health issues do commit antisocial acts, mental health issues do not equal criminality or violence – despite the media's tendency to emphasize a suspected link. People with mental health issues are no more likely to commit violence than any one in the general public, but they are more likely to be victimized and are more likely to inflict violent behaviors on themselves.

Myth: Mental health issues happen because of bad parenting or personal weakness.

Fact: The main risk factors for mental health issues are not bad parenting or personal weakness but rather genetics, severe and prolonged stress (such as physical or sexual abuse), or other environmental influences (such as birth trauma or head injury).

Myth: Treatments for mental health issues are not usually effective.

Fact: The effectiveness of any treatment depends on a number of factors including the type of mental health issue and the particular needs of the individual. A combination of psychiatric medication and psychotherapy, or social interventions are the most effective way to treat mental health issues.

Myth: Mental health conditions are caused by everyday stressors.

Fact: It may seem that stress is responsible for mental health conditions; however, there is no one clear cause of mental health issues. Rather, it is a result of complex interactions between psychological, biological, genetic and social factors. Stress, stigma, and lack of support can make it worse on the individual.

Myth: Mental health issues are always hereditary.

Fact: Some mental health issues include a genetic component, which results in a predisposition or vulnerability toward the mental health problems among children and siblings, but environment also plays a key role in the development of certain conditions. If someone in one's family has a mental health condition, that person will be at higher risk.

If you start to experience the symptoms of a mental health condition, it is important for you to see a mental health professional to determine if you have a problem that will require treatment. If you know of anyone who seems to have symptoms of a mental health condition, urge them to do the same.

Coping with the Stigma of a Mental Health Issue

Get treatment. Don't let the fear of being labeled with a mental health issue prevent you from seeking help. Treatment can provide relief by identifying and reducing symptoms that interfere with your work and personal life. How can you get treatment? _____

_____

_____

_____

Don't let stigma create self-doubt and shame. If you are buying into the stigma, you will have the mistaken belief that your condition is a sign of personal weakness, or that you should be able to control it better. How can you have less self-doubt? _____

_____

_____

_____

How can you have less shame? _____

_____

_____

_____

Don't isolate yourself. Have the courage to confide in your family members, friends, dating partner, clergy, school counselor or other members of your groups and/or community. Who can you reach out to and who can you trust for the compassion, support and understanding you need? _____

_____

_____

_____

Remember that you are not your issue. So instead of saying "I am a moody person," say "I am a person with varied moods." In what ways do you equate yourself with your mood issue? _____

_____

_____

_____

Get help at school. If you are having mood disturbances or mood swings that affect your learning, find out what plans and programs might help. Who could you talk to about getting help at your school? _____

_____

_____

_____

If you and others are willing, share responses.

Erasing the Stigma of Mental Health Issues

Speak Out Against Stigmas

It can help instill courage in others who are facing mood disturbances, it will help to educate the public about the effect that these mood swings have on you personally. Speaking out for, and about, yourself advocates for others who might have mood issues and it can be beneficial to you at the same time. Think about some of the ways that you might let your voice be heard about stigmas and their damaging effects on people. For each of the items, list the ways that you could speak out against stigmas.

Express your opinions at events. What events are planned at your school where you might speak out against stigmas? _____

_____

_____

At what events in your community might you volunteer to speak out against stigmas? _____

_____

_____

You could write an informative feature article or letter to the editor of a local newspaper or your school newspaper. What would you say? _____

_____

_____

You could blog about stigmas on the Internet. How can you do this? _____

_____

_____

What are some other ways to speak out against stigmas? _____

_____

_____

How do you think this will benefit others? _____

_____

_____

How will it benefit you? _____

_____

_____

Whole Person Associates is the leading publisher of training resources for professionals who empower people to create and maintain healthy lifestyles. Our creative resources will help you work effectively with your clients in the areas of stress management, wellness promotion, mental health and life skills.

Please visit us at our web site: **www.wholeperson.com**. You can check out our entire line of products, place an order, request our print catalog, and sign up for our monthly special notifications.

Whole Person Associates

800-247-6789